T0196109

An Analysis of

Karen Z. Ho's

Liquidated
An Ethnography of Wall Street

Rodolfo Maggio

Published by Macat International Ltd
24:13 Coda Centre, 189 Munster Road, London SW6 6AW.

Distributed exclusively by Routledge
2 Park Square, Milton Park, Abingdon, Oxon OX14 4RN
711 Third Avenue, New York, NY 10017, USA

Routledge is an imprint of the Taylor & Francis Group, an informa business

www.macat.com
info@macat.com

Cataloguing in Publication Data
A catalogue record for this book is available from the British Library.
Library of Congress Cataloguing-in-Publication Data is available upon request.
Cover illustration: Etienne Gilfillan

ISBN 978-1-912302-07-9 (hardback)
ISBN 978-1-912128-06-8 (paperback)
ISBN 978-1-912128-32-7 (e-book)

Notice
The information in this book is designed to orientate readers of the work under analysis,
to elucidate and contextualise its key ideas and themes, and to aid in the development
of critical thinking skills. It is not meant to be used, nor should it be used, as a
substitute for original thinking or in place of original writing or research. References and
notes are provided for informational purposes and their presence does not constitute
endorsement of the information or opinions therein. This book is presented solely for
educational purposes. It is sold on the understanding that the publisher is not engaged
to provide any scholarly advice. The publisher has made every effort to ensure that
this book is accurate and up-to-date, but makes no warranties or representations with
regard to the completeness or reliability of the information it contains. The information
and the opinions provided herein are not guaranteed or warranted to produce particular
results and may not be suitable for students of every ability. The publisher shall not be
liable for any loss, damage or disruption arising from any errors or omissions, or from
the use of this book, including, but not limited to, special, incidental, consequential or
other damages caused, or alleged to have been caused, directly or indirectly, by the
information contained within.

CONTENTS

THE MACAT LIBRARY

The Macat Library is a series of unique academic explorations of seminal works in the humanities and social sciences – books and papers that have had a significant and widely recognised impact on their disciplines. It has been created to serve as much more than just a summary of what lies between the covers of a great book. It illuminates and explores the influences on, ideas of, and impact of that book. Our goal is to offer a learning resource that encourages critical thinking and fosters a better, deeper understanding of important ideas.

Each publication is divided into three Sections: Influences, Ideas, and Impact. Each Section has four Modules. These explore every important facet of the work, and the responses to it.

This Section-Module structure makes a Macat Library book easy to use, but it has another important feature. Because each Macat book is written to the same format, it is possible (and encouraged!) to cross-reference multiple Macat books along the same lines of inquiry or research. This allows the reader to open up interesting interdisciplinary pathways.

To further aid your reading, lists of glossary terms and people mentioned are included at the end of this book (these are indicated by an asterisk [*] throughout) – as well as a list of works cited.

Macat has worked with the University of Cambridge to identify the elements of critical thinking and understand the ways in which six different skills combine to enable effective thinking.
Three allow us to fully understand a problem; three more give us the tools to solve it. Together, these six skills make up the **PACIER** model of critical thinking. They are:

ANALYSIS – understanding how an argument is built
EVALUATION – exploring the strengths and weaknesses of an argument
INTERPRETATION – understanding issues of meaning

CREATIVE THINKING – coming up with new ideas and fresh connections
PROBLEM-SOLVING – producing strong solutions
REASONING – creating strong arguments

To find out more, visit **WWW.MACAT.COM.**

CRITICAL THINKING AND *LIQUIDATED*

Primary critical thinking skill: PROBLEM SOLVING
Secondary critical thinking skill: CREATIVE THINKING

Liquidated is a work of anthropology that treats an unusual, despised subculture – that of the Wall Street banker – much as anthropologists have traditionally treated remote 'savage' tribes. But using the techniques of ethnography, including interviews, analysis of daily lives, and fieldwork to investigate a modern western culture is not original; what sets Ho's work apart and gives it value is her mastery of the critical thinking skills of problem-solving and creative thinking to reconceptualize the way in which we understand the bankers' mindset.

Ho's great achievement is to ask productive questions, most obviously in drawing a distinction between bankers' self-image as capitalist warriors, freeing up value for themselves and shareholders by increasing the liquidity of the assets they invest in, and the social consequences of what they do. As Ho points out, not only is Wall Street institutionally inclined to embrace risk, in order to maximise profit; it is also prone to assume that increased liquidity (most often achieved by breaking up and selling off the parts of a large corporation) is good in itself, irrespective of the outcomes for the workers actually involved in these disposals. Considering alternative possibilities, and generating fresh solutions, Ho determines that the capitalist principles that underpin Wall Street are myths, not the expression of some natural economic law.

ABOUT THE AUTHOR OF THE ORIGINAL WORK

Karen Z. Ho is a contemporary Taiwanese American anthropologist. Born in Chiayi in southwest Taiwan in 1971, she grew up in the US state of Tennessee before her studies took her first to Stanford, then to Princeton.

Ho took a sabbatical from academia to get an insider's view of the world of high finance, and went to work in an investment bank at the heart of the industry in New York. Six months later, she was dismissed when entire departments were closed as part of a major corporate restructuring. This experience, and the questions it inspired, became the basis for her PhD, which would later become her most celebrated published work, 2009's *Liquidated: An Ethnography of Wall Street*. She is now a member of the department of anthropology at the University of Minnesota.

ABOUT THE AUTHOR OF THE ANALYSIS

Dr Rodolfo Maggio holds a masters degree in anthropology from the London School of Economics and a PhD in social anthropology from the University of Manchester. He is currently a postdoctoral researcher in the Department of Psychiatry at the University of Oxford.

ABOUT MACAT

GREAT WORKS FOR CRITICAL THINKING

Macat is focused on making the ideas of the world's great thinkers accessible and comprehensible to everybody, everywhere, in ways that promote the development of enhanced critical thinking skills.

It works with leading academics from the world's top universities to produce new analyses that focus on the ideas and the impact of the most influential works ever written across a wide variety of academic disciplines. Each of the works that sit at the heart of its growing library is an enduring example of great thinking. But by setting them in context – and looking at the influences that shaped their authors, as well as the responses they provoked – Macat encourages readers to look at these classics and game-changers with fresh eyes. Readers learn to think, engage and challenge their ideas, rather than simply accepting them.

"Macat offers an amazing first-of-its-kind tool for interdisciplinary learning and research. Its focus on works that transformed their disciplines and its rigorous approach, drawing on the world's leading experts and educational institutions, opens up a world-class education to anyone."

Andreas Schleicher
Director for Education and Skills, Organisation for Economic Co-operation and Development

'Macat is taking on some of the major challenges in university education ... They have drawn together a strong team of active academics who are producing teaching materials that are novel in the breadth of their approach.'

Prof Lord Broers,
former Vice-Chancellor of the University of Cambridge

'The Macat vision is exceptionally exciting. It focuses upon new modes of learning which analyse and explain seminal texts which have profoundly influenced world thinking and so social and economic development. It promotes the kind of critical thinking which is essential for any society and economy. This is the learning of the future.'

Rt Hon Charles Clarke, former UK Secretary of State for Education

'The Macat analyses provide immediate access to the critical conversation surrounding the books that have shaped their respective discipline, which will make them an invaluable resource to all of those, students and teachers, working in the field.'

Professor William Tronzo, University of California at San Diego

WAYS IN TO THE TEXT

KEY POINTS

- Karen Z. Ho is an American anthropologist. Applying the principles of ethnographic* research (systematic observation of a people in the field), she conducted research on people working in the world of finance and corporate business in the United States ("Wall Street"),* considering them to be a distinct subculture.
- *Liquidated* (2009) is a detailed description of the world view, beliefs, and practices of Wall Street culture, which centers on precarious conditions and high risk, ultimately leading to financial crises.
- Ho's work contributes to public debates about the underlying causes of contemporary financial crises, and advances the growing field of the anthropology* of money and finance. Anthropology is the study of human beings (commonly society, beliefs, and cultural practices).

Who Is Karen Z. Ho?

Karen Zouwen Ho, the author of *Liquidated: An Ethnography of Wall Street* (2009), was born in Chiayi in southwest Taiwan in 1971 to parents of Taiwanese origin, and grew up in the US state of Tennessee. She studied anthropology as an undergraduate at Stanford University in California, conducting her graduate studies at Princeton, eventually taking up a PhD in social anthropology* (the comparative study of human societies). During the first year of her PhD she became interested in Wall Street, both the site of the central US stock market and the seat of American corporate and finance culture. In order to explore the distinct values and practices there, and their consequences to wider society, Ho took a leave from Princeton to work in a bank.

Experiencing Wall Street life on a daily basis allowed certain paradoxes to emerge in her mind and encouraged her to reconsider some of the basic assumptions about this significant, but often misunderstood, part of society. After six months she was sacked when her department was closed to cut costs as part of a restructuring of the bank (a policy called "downsizing").* Simultaneously, the company's stock prices went up. This was puzzling; logically, it seemed to Ho that these layoffs would have signaled that the company was in bad shape and prompted a drop in the stock price. Wanting to explore this seeming contradiction, Ho asked whether it could be explained as a causal link between downsizing and shareholder value* (the wealth earned by the owners of a company's stocks).

Currently, Ho works in the department of anthropology at the University of Minnesota, teaching anthropology of capitalism,* finance, and globalization.*"Capitalism" refers to the social and economic system dominant in the West, in which trade and industry are held in private hands and conducted for private profit, "globalization" refers to the commercial, political, and social ties across international borders that increasingly define the modern world.

Ho is married, and has a daughter and a son. The book is dedicated to them, "in the hope that their generation will see greater socioeconomic equality."[1]

What Does *Liquidated* Say?

As anticipated in the subtitle *An Ethnography of Wall Street*, Karen Ho's *Liquidated* uses the strategies and techniques that ethnographers have traditionally used to study other cultures in order to generate a better understanding of Wall Street. It is a detailed description of the everyday lives of investment bankers,* with a focus on their world view, practices, and beliefs. In this world, raising the value of company stock is a paramount priority, and risky financial strategies are central to maintaining the upward climb of shareholder value, even though these practices mean that Wall Street is constantly flirting with financial crashes.

While this might seem contradictory, Karen Ho shows that, from the point of view of an insider, it is perfectly reasonable. Wall Street investment bankers are socially conditioned to take risky decisions and to consider uncertainty and constant pressure as an inevitable part of the terrain in the world of finance. High earning prospects provide a powerful incentive to endure and thrive in these conditions, along with the unfailing belief that they are the smartest, most hardworking, and best connected agents of the global economy.

Ho could see the importance of this particular belief system and investigated how it becomes firmly instilled in the minds of Wall Streeters. Initially, Wall Street employers recruit their employees from prestigious ("Ivy League") universities where ideas of excellence and privilege are already present; finance and corporate employers consolidate these ideas, celebrating these students as the best, the smartest, and brightest. Rituals including expensive dinners in luxury restaurants strengthen their self-image as members of an elite.

For those who land a job, the reality of Wall Street life proves far less glamorous. Working up to 100 hours per week under the constant risk of sudden downsizing is common, particularly for new recruits. In their view, however, these taxing conditions build character and confirm their sense of superiority. It is seen as a necessary step in transforming students and junior workers into proper bankers, equipped to make a lot of money quickly, and who are always ready to move swiftly on to their next job. Like a commodity or financial asset that can be easily bought, sold, or converted into cash, their very lives have become *liquid*.

This way of life, and the beliefs that underpin it, constitute Wall Street's culture of liquidity;* taken to its furthest extreme, "liquidity" means transforming everything into a commodity (something which can be traded) and increasing the speed at which it is sold. In particular, the stocks of a company get very close to the purest form of value when they can be traded at maximum liquidity. Therefore, since the 1980s, it has become increasingly common for investors to buy a company when its stock price is low, with the sole objective of increasing the price of its stocks and making a profit. Rather than taking measures to improve the long-term performance of the company itself, these new owners have tended to take actions to increase the stock value, often breaking up the companies they buy in order to realize their ideal of liquidity. This kind of practice is one of the key causes of large-scale financial collapses and the social problems that accompany them. Oddly, people working in the financial sector persistently believe that increasing the liquidity of a company means making it more efficient, and are largely unconcerned with the consequences of their financial strategies on society as a whole.

Crises, Ho concludes, are not the result of inbuilt "natural" cycles of the financial market (the idea that "what goes up must come down"); she shows, rather, that financial crashes are the realization of the bankers' ideal of ultimate liquidity.

Why Does *Liquidated* Matter?

In the aftermath of the global 2007–8 financial crisis, a contentious debate took place about the causes of the meltdown. In the past, massive financial crashes of this kind were usually explained as inevitable stages in market cycles. For Karen Ho, these popular explanations distance the crises from the financial centers—and the people in them—that generate crises.

Ho argues that abstract discussions and approaches that treat the financial market like a force of nature cannot answer the question,

"Who caused the crisis?" Grounded analyses of investment banking practices, however, can answer the question, showing that financial meltdowns happen because financial bankers produce them.

With so many people suffering from the consequences of the 2007–8 crash, *Liquidated* contributes to a debate of real public relevance. It is a solid piece of ethnographic writing that explores the daily practices of financial bankers and goes some way to explaining the repercussions of Wall Street culture on society at large. Some readers outside the field of anthropology, however, might find *Liquidated* a tough read; Ho uses technical, ethnographic terminology and slants her work towards a long-standing debate in the field of economic anthropology* (the study of human economic behavior). Still, *Liquidated* has contributed significantly to its field, proposing a structured way to investigate the culture of Wall Street and global financial capitalism from an anthropological perspective. Capitalism is an economic and social system in which trade, production, and investment are held in private hands and conducted for private profit.

The practices of the financial sector have the profound potential to affect and disrupt the daily lives of ordinary people around the world. This link has drawn increasing numbers of anthropologists to look at finance more closely through the field of economic anthropology, and its subfield, the anthropology of money and finance. Few anthropologists have illustrated the link between Wall Street culture and financial crises as successfully and comprehensively as Karen Ho, lending *Liquidated* a particular importance in the field of economic anthropology today.

Since its publication in 2009, *Liquidated* has generated a great deal of interest. In particular, specialists on issues such as the value of risk and market temporalities*—the way in which the rhythms, agendas, and events in the world of finance produce a distinct perception of time—were drawn to the book. Anthropologists of money and finance have praised it almost unanimously, considering it a major point of reference with the potential to become a classic of economic anthropology.

NOTES

1   Karen Z. Ho, *Liquidated: An Ethnography of Wall Street* (Durham: Duke University Press, 2009), v.

SECTION 1
INFLUENCES

MODULE 1
THE AUTHOR AND THE HISTORICAL CONTEXT

KEY POINTS

- Karen Z. Ho wrote *Liquidated* (2009) in order to investigate the influence of the Wall Street* culture of liquidity* on the American financial market and society as well as its repercussions on other global societies and institutions ("Wall Street" is the financial center of the United States; "liquidity" is the measure of the speed at which something can be bought or sold in the market without affecting the price).

- *Liquidated* interweaves Ho's interests in the relationship between financial markets and society, her studies in anthropology* (the study of human beings, commonly human culture, society, and belief) and her experience of working for, and being laid off by, a financial institution.

- Ho's work counters the popular perception of financial markets as being regulated by abstract laws, representing them instead as governed by powerful players whose decisions influence society at large.

Why Read This Text?

Karen Z. Ho wrote *Liquidated: An Ethnography of Wall Street* (2009) in order to shed light on the causes of contemporary economic crises. Her interest in Wall Street culture was kindled by the financial turmoil that has hit American society periodically over the past 30 years. In order to investigate these issues, she used ethnographic* methods (methods of conducting research on a specific group of people in the field) and showed that economic crises are not inevitable, but socially constructed by Wall Street financial bankers.

❝ The moment appeared rife with ethnographic significance: financiers, the instigators of mass corporate restructurings throughout the United States, were downsizing themselves. BT's loss was ironically the anthropologist's gain. These seemingly mundane experiences of downsizing and job insecurity, everyday occurrences at investment banks, might yield crucial insights into the contemporary moment of financial crises and globalization. ❞

Karen Z. Ho, *Liquidated: An Ethnography of Wall Street*

She discovered that it is the culture of Wall Street that predisposes financial bankers to cause financial crises. It does so by shaping the role of the banker to be fundamentally characterized by taking high-risk decisions in an extremely unstable market and precarious workplace. Knowingly, regardless of the negative repercussions on society, they value liquidity above anything else. In other words, they are culturally predisposed to create crises.

These conclusions are relevant for both the academic community and the general public. According to the British anthropologist of economic behavior Keith Hart,* *Liquidated* "seems to mark a coming of age for the contemporary discipline,"[1] the anthropology of money and finance. As for the impact on US society, Ho challenges the popular misconception of financial crises as the inevitable consequences of "natural" market structures that individuals are powerless to control, and proposes an explanation couched in real-life practices and cultural norms.

The influence of Wall Street culture, however, is not limited to the American financial market and society. Booms, busts, failures, and credit crunches have repercussions that reach every corner of the world as a consequence of the global interconnections of financial markets and societies. It follows that the observations and conclusions Ho offers in *Liquidated* are relevant not only in the context of the 2007–8 financial crash, or the economic downturn that followed it. Ho's study has also helped improve the general understanding of the evolution of the global financial economy.

Author's Life

Karen Z. Ho was born in Chiayi, Taiwan in 1971. She grew up near Memphis, Tennessee and did her undergraduate studies at Stanford University and her graduate studies at Princeton. An anthropologist to the core, Ho has an innate drive to understand people and their culture, and this has consistently guided her life choices and influenced the ways she interprets the world, including Wall Street and investment banking.*

In 1995, news of major restructuring at the American telecommunications giant AT&T* caught her attention and led directly to the formation of her research question. As she recounts in the introduction to *Liquidated*, "AT&T had just announced that it would split into three different companies, engendering one of the largest dismantlings of a corporation in US history: 77,800 managers received 'buy-out offers' and 48,500 workers were downsized." "Downsizing" here is a euphemism for "sacked": they lost their jobs because the company wanted to reduce costs. She observed that rather than shrinking the value of the company's stock, "on the first day of the announcement, AT&T stock leaped 6.125 points to 63.75, or 10.6 percent of its total value, 'growing' another $9.7 billion. But what shocked me the most, upon further investigation, was that the stock prices of Wall Street investment banks also rose."[2] Ho was motivated to understand the reasons behind this apparent contradiction.

Eager to find an answer, in 1996 Ho took part in the recruitment process of the spring career services "at Princeton University, a recruiting hotbed for investment banks."[3] She gained a position as an internal management consultant at Bankers Trust New York

Corporation (BT),* providing her with hands-on experience of financial banking. She planned to return to graduate school, in order to study the culture of Wall Street, after a substantial period working at BT. But in January 1997, BT managers eliminated her department in order to reduce costs and raise shareholder value* (the wealth earned by the owners of a company's stocks), and her employment was terminated after only six months. Fatefully, she had just experienced a process that stood at the core of her research question: the relationship between downsizing and shareholder value.[4]

In order to investigate this connection, Ho designed an ethnographic research project. A year after her downsizing, she began 17 months of fieldwork among investment bankers working in some of the major Wall Street financial institutions. On the basis of her research on the culture of Wall Street, she wrote her dissertation and received her PhD in anthropology from Princeton University. *Liquidated*, her first book, is mostly based on her doctoral dissertation.

Author's Background

In the 1980s, many major American corporations were attempting to cut costs and raise shareholder value by reducing their investments in research development and infrastructure, thereby rendering many people jobless. Rising unemployment and other negative consequences of corporate downsizing became an increasing contributor to traumatic social and economic inequalities. Confronted with these painful events—first in other people's lives and later in her own experience—Ho decided to apply the methods of anthropological research to understand what motivates this dramatic corporate downsizing and causes financial crises.

Financial crises are often interpreted as the inevitable consequences of the way deregulated, privatized "neoliberal"* markets work; evidence of the dominance of the deterministic* position that sees markets broadly as governed by a set of abstract, predetermined, laws. Such interpretations tend to justify the ups and downs of the economy as in-built, structural features, rather than pointing to a causal link between corporate strategies and the culture of Wall Street, and socioeconomic inequality beyond the world of finance.

Ho believes that the tendency to explain crises as inevitable consequences of neoliberal market logics prevents us from identifying the powerful players who are responsible for the socioeconomic inequalities produced by financial crises. Furthermore, the deterministic perception just described is also preventing corrective action against future crises. Ho's solution is to illustrate that crises do not simply happen like dramatic weather events; they are the product of a chain reaction connecting socioeconomic inequality to corporate strategies generated by the culture of Wall Street.

NOTES

1   Keith Hart, "Review of *Liquidated: An Ethnography of Wall Street* by Karen Ho," *American Ethnologist* 38, no. 2 (May 1, 2011): 378–9.

2   Karen Z. Ho, *Liquidated: An Ethnography of Wall Street* (Durham: Duke University Press, 2009), 13–14.

3   Ho, *Liquidated*, 1.

4   Ho, *Liquidated*, 13–17.

MODULE 2
ACADEMIC CONTEXT

KEY POINTS

- *Liquidated* is a significant recent contribution to economic anthropology,* a field of study concerned with the ways in which economies are embedded in social and cultural practices.

- The anthropology of money and finance has been growing along with the important role of financial institutions in the globalized* world. This has resulted in an increasing number of ethnographies of finance (studies of the people who work in the financial world).

- Karen Z. Ho borrowed the concept of "habitus"* (a word relating to the relation between personality and the individual's social or cultural context) from the French sociologist Pierre Bourdieu* in order to illustrate how Wall Street* investment bankers* create and perpetuate socioeconomic inequality.

The Work in its Context

Karen Z. Ho's *Liquidated: An Ethnography of Wall Street,* her first book, is one of the latest developments in the relatively new subfield of economic anthropology: the anthropology of finance. She joins a growing number of anthropologists who, as Ho puts it, "[at] last overcame their inhibitions concerning the study of money."[1]

In the heyday of economic anthropology at the beginning of the twentieth century, the Hungarian American economist Karl P. Polanyi* observed that through history, societies have tended to produce a particular kind of economy that reflects its stage of social evolution. In more primitive societies, the economy has tended to be more

> ❝ High finance is largely concerned with personalities, private perks and little interest groups, prestige, imagination, almost anything but what might be called a market. ❞
>
> Daniel Miller, "Turning Callon the Right Way Up," *Economy and Society*

"embedded" into the social structure; further along the evolutionary stages, the economic sector of society becomes less "embedded" and increasingly separated from the rest of its culture and society.[2] Economic anthropologists, however, argued against this formalist*idea—that is, the idea of impersonal, disembodied, abstract markets that operate on similar lines regardless of social context. In contrast, they defended the "substantivist"* notion, according to which *all* forms of economy are embedded in and dependent on social relations.[3]

Since the 1980s, the substantivist perspective on money in society has attracted many prominent anthropologists, among them Chris Gregory,* Keith Hart,* Joel Robbins,* Maurice Bloch,* and David Akin.* In the subfield of economic anthropology, anthropologists of finance soon began to appear, such as Bill Maurer,* Mitchel Abolafia,* Ellen Hertz,* and Hirokazu Miyazaki.* Their individual researches are underscored by a common approach: they all apply the substantivist model to the contemporary study of finance. In so doing, they culturalize finance, reiterating that there is no such a thing as the *homo economicus**— the "economic man" (as distinct from ordinary people), who is driven solely by crude self-interest—as formalist theories would argue.

These and other anthropologists of finance have shown that culture and society, rather than abstract economic models, influence the way financial actors behave. However, as Keith Hart points out, many of the studies produced to date "are quite traditional in their focus, being concerned with the traders' local practices and point of view, even if the object of their business is global at another level."[4] The work of Karen Ho inherits the substantivist tradition and aims to connect the culture of Wall Street to global finance.

Overview of the Field

In the field of economic anthropology, ethnographers of finance look to the unique culture of the finance world for evidence to disprove the assumption that financial markets are governed by abstract principles of neoclassical economics* such as profit maximization, money meritocracy* (the idea that the hardest workers will be the biggest earners), and rational choice. They are concerned with demonstrating that market laws are neither universal human traits nor the economic counterpart of natural laws that people are powerless to control. They focus on practices embedded in and informed by specific cultural traits of particular groups, such as Wall Street investment bankers.

In his pioneering ethnography* of Wall Street *Making Markets*, the social scientist Mitchel Abolafia looks at stocks, bonds, and futures markets as elements of a culture, rather than mere financial instruments* (bonds, stocks, derivatives, and other things that can be traded).[5] Rather than applying a simplistic, abstract notion of self-interested, profit-maximizing individuals, Abolafia describes New York Stock Exchange specialists as constantly negotiating their position along a tension that opposes short-term self-interest with long-term self-restraint. In so doing, he contributes to making the anthropological point that there is no such thing as a natural desire for profit, but only practices that reinforce ideas, beliefs, and a specific cultural predisposition with which financial actors identify.

The professor of anthropology and international studies Hirokazu Miyazaki conducted ethnographic research with a group of Japanese traders. He demonstrated that they experience a distinct and peculiar sense of time because of the competing temporal demands of securities trading with markets across vastly different time zones on one hand, and the local Japanese workplace on the other.[6] The implications of these temporal incompatibilities can have a major impact on financial trade centers and beyond. For example, Ho found that one particular manifestation of market temporality* (the relation to time unique to the market) on Wall Street was the tendency of investment banks to downsize* their workforces—that is, sack people to cut costs—in order to meet expectations dictated by quarterly efficiency goals.

Academic Influences

The concept of *habitus* developed by the French sociologist Pierre Bourdieu served as a key part of Ho's methodology in her interpretation of Wall Street culture. Developed across a number of Bourdieu's works on social inequality, the concept refers to a set of conditions that predispose an individual to function in a given social context and to interpret it in a particular way.

The structures of the habitus operate as principles that generate and organize both representations (simply, the way things are represented in images, language, and so on) and practices. In a somewhat circular logic, these practices are constructed in a manner that means they accord with the specific consequences of holding the world view associated with that habitus. That is to say: these practices both project an individual's subjective world view (the world view unique to the individual) onto the outside world and structure the world in the individual's own image.

Bourdieu developed the concept of habitus from his study of a number of previous thinkers—from the ancient Greek philosopher Aristotle* to the twentieth-century French sociologist Marcel Mauss*—in order to highlight social inequalities in the French education system. He used it to demonstrate that social classes create their own class habitus. Most importantly, he demonstrated that French elites, by reproducing their habitus in the process of acculturation* (through which a person acquires the culture of a different group as a consequence of being in contact with its members), simultaneously reproduce inequality through their practices. Ho applies Bourdieu's concept of habitus to analyze and explain the behavior of investment bankers. Her objective is to demonstrate the influence of their particular predispositions on practices intended to raise the value of shares, such as downsizing, selling off units, and meeting Wall Street quarterly objectives regardless of the human costs. It follows that these practices bear heavy implications for society at large. This pursuit of efficiency through downsizing influences American life in many aspects today, notably by continuing to bring about inequality.

NOTES

1   Keith Hart, "Review of *Liquidated: An Ethnography of Wall Street* by Karen Ho," *American Ethnologist* 38, no. 2 (May 1, 2011): 378.

2   Karl Polanyi, *The Great Transformation: The Political and Economic Origins of Our Time* (Boston: Beacon Press, 1944).

3   George Dalton, "Economic Theory and Primitive Society," *American Anthropologist* 63, no. 1 (1961): 1–25; Marshall Sahlins, *Stone Age Economics* (New York: Aldine, 1972); Stephen Gudeman, *Economics as Culture: Models and Metaphors of Livelihood* (Boston: Routledge and Kegan Paul, 1986); James G. Carrier, ed., *Meanings of the Market: The Free Market in Western Culture* (Oxford: Berg, 1997); Daniel Miller, "Turning Callon the Right Way Up," *Economy and Society* 31, no. 2 (2002): 218–33.

4   Keith Hart, "Contemporary Research on the Anthropology of Money and Finance," *The Memory Bank,* September 4, 2013, accessed October 9, 2015, http://thememorybank.co.uk/2013/09/04/contemporary-research-on-the-anthropology-of-money-and-finance/.

5   Mitchel Abolafia, *Making Markets: Opportunism and Restraint on Wall Street* (Cambridge, Mass.: Harvard University Press, 2001).

6   Hirokazu Miyazaki, "The Temporalities of the Market," *American Anthropologist* 105, no. 2 (2003): 255–65.

MODULE 3
THE PROBLEM

KEY POINTS

- At the core of *Liquidated* is a question about the connection between shareholder value* and corporate restructuring, and about the best methodology for studying financial institutions.

- Participants in the debate about how best to understand economics, society, and culture take positions along a scale between the theoretical approaches of formalism* (according to which, roughly, economies operate according to the similar goals of those engaging in economic behavior) and substantivism* (according to which economic behavior is influenced by sociocultural factors that vary from context to context).

- Ho's approach further refines the substantivist position by showing that, in finance, models and practices are inextricably linked.

Core Question

At the core of Karen Ho's *Liquidated: An Ethnography of Wall Street* is a question about the connection between shareholder value and corporate restructuring: Why do stock prices rise when corporations begin to downsize* their employees and sell off their units? Initially, the relationship seems counterintuitive. Should not the dismantling of a corporation be interpreted as a bad moment and result in a decrease in the value of its stocks?

Answering this question required Karen Z. Ho to immerse herself in the culture of Wall Street* investment bankers.* There she observed a positive perception of these forms of corporate dismantling as signals

> 66 How can I account for the fact that even when
> my informants realized that a particular corporate
> restructuring they advised was not a 'solid deal'—
> that it could result in shareholder value decline (and
> be detrimental according to other socioeconomic
> parameters)—they still pushed the deal through and
> continued to use shareholder value as justification?
> How are they called upon to both downsize
> corporate America (and themselves) and detract from
> shareholder value? 99
>
> Karen Z. Ho, *Liquidated: An Ethnography of Wall Street*

that the particular corporation is becoming leaner, more financially efficient, more *liquid*. "Liquidity"* is the measure of the speed at which a commodity is bought or sold in the market without affecting the price; for Wall Street insiders, it leads to a rise in stock prices.

In many cases, however, shareholder value declines as a consequence of a bad deal. Even when it is clear that the financial strategy is not going to result in raising stock prices, Wall Street investment bankers still push the deal through and persist in using shareholder value as a justification. This odd phenomenon led Ho to realize that "the model of shareholder value, despite its role as Wall Street's moral blueprint, could not fully explain how investment bankers were propelled to seemingly contradict their own value system." She looked to the culture of Wall Street to seek out the other factors that might account for the persistence of "the presumed correlation between constantly rising stock prices and downsizings [which] often broke down under the weight of bad deals and poor strategies, leading more to financial booms, busts, and fiascos than 'actual' shareholder value."[1]

The Participants

The questions at the core of *Liquidated* are part of a longstanding debate between the formalist* interpretation, which views financial crises as a part of economic cycles, and substantivist* conceptions, which view the economy as driven by people and their cultural norms. For substantivists, the behavior of investment bankers who consciously push bad deals through cannot be considered rational according to neoclassical* notions of utility.* According to neoclassical economics, resources are allocated according to the use of available knowledge, rational choice, and the independent action of individuals; "utility" refers to the satisfaction or advantage experienced in return for an economic action.

Karen Ho takes a typically substantive position to explain the behavior of investment bankers, approaching the subject by immersing herself in the particular culture of Wall Street rather than by studying neoclassical economic models.

Karl P. Polanyi* is often referred to as the scholar who first challenged the formalist assumption that neoclassical economic models could be universally applied. He proposed instead that non-Western, pre-modern economies were deeply embedded in social relations, while contemporary, Western market economies are more separated from social relations. His position presumed a radical opposition between Western and non-Western societies that later anthropologists challenged.

The social scientists Don Slater* and Fran Tonkiss* argued that it is incorrect to assume that premodern economies (which do not operate according to market principles as they are understood in the developed world), are the only ones to be embedded in social relations, whereas modern industrial economies operate according to abstract economic models. "Just as 'nonmarket' gift exchanges [in non-Western societies] are characterized by a high degree of formal calculation, 'market economies are more fully embedded in social networks than Polanyi's strict separation allows.'"[2] From Slater and Tonkiss's radical substantivist position, *all* economies should be understood as deeply dependent on the sociocultural institutions of their context.

An economy, in other words, cannot be considered as separate from the practices, norms, and values that define a society.

Anthropologists such as Marshall Sahlins* and Stephen Gudeman* also defended the substantivist positions, although they mostly studied non-Western societies. Recently, an increasing number of economic anthropologists,* among them Mitchel Abolafia,* Karen Ho, and Rebecca Cassidy,* shifted the focus to Western societies. In so doing, they were responding to anthropologist Laura Nader's* call for the field to *study up*,* in other words to analyze the dominant and powerful groups, "the colonizers rather than the colonized."[3] This involved subjecting financial institutions to a similar ethnographic* scrutiny that the field had begun to apply to other parts of Western society.

The Contemporary Debate

In recent years, there has been considerable anthropological reflection on the social and economic system of capitalism,* neoliberalism* (a set of capitalist theories that support privatization, deregulation, free trade, and the enhancement of the private sector at the expense of the public sector) and Western financial markets.[4] Recent ethnographic studies of people working in corporations and investment banks demonstrate that financial markets are socially constructed and produced according to specific cultural practices.[5] An increasing number of researchers, including Ho, are looking to this culture to unravel the root causes of financial crises.

Arguably, scholars such as Giovanni Arrighi* and Philip McMichael* still tend to frame contemporary Western economies in terms of abstract financial models and universalist* notions of globalized* markets that are becoming increasingly similar ("universalism" is the theoretical position that a particular generalization applies to all cases). According to them, the economy has become dis-embedded from society (that is, free from social norms and practices) as a consequence of the implementation of Western-style neoliberal capitalism on a global scale.[6] It follows that, even though they consider it misleading to assume that economic principles inform economic practices rather than the other way around, they argue that these practices eventually construct all-encompassing economic models that are adopted globally, leading to a standardization of world economies.

Opponents of this stance include the social scientist Michel Callon,* who criticized the British anthropologist Daniel Miller* for abstracting (that is, over-theorizing) financial economic models and theories, arguing instead that economic subjects—that is, real people interacting with the economy—construct economic models and theories as daily practices.[7]

Ho, however, contends that both Miller and Callon are wrong to assume a separation between models and practices in the first place. If she were to take this view, she would not have been able to interpret shareholder value as justification for the culture of liquidity. Rather, she would be bound "to see the current dominance of shareholder value as evidence either that *homo economicus** now exists, as financial economics has converged with market practices, *or* that market mechanisms have abstracted social relations according to virtual, utopian capitalist fantasies."[8] "*Homo economicus*"— economic man— denotes humans not prone to irrational behaviors, always focused on maximizing their gains.

Or, to put it more simply, Ho contends that, as far as economies in general are concerned, models and practices cannot be separated: each plays a defining role in the constitution of the other.

NOTES

1   Karen Z. Ho, *Liquidated: An Ethnography of Wall Street* (Durham: Duke University Press, 2009), 168.

2   Ho, *Liquidated,* 32.

3   Laura Nader, "Up the Anthropologist—Perspectives Gained from Studying Up," in *Reinventing Anthropology,* ed. Dell Hymes (New York: Pantheon Books, 1972), 289.

4   James Carrier, ed. *Meanings of the Market: The Free Market in Western Culture* (Oxford: Berg, 1997).

5   Mitchel Abolafia, *Making Markets: Opportunism and Restraint on Wall Street* (Cambridge, Mass.: Harvard University Press, 2001).

6   Philip McMichael, "Development and Structural Adjustment," in *Virtualism: A New Political Economy,* ed. James G. Carrier and Daniel Miller (Oxford: Berg, 1998), 95–116; Giovanni Arrighi, *The Long Twentieth Century: Money, Power, and the Origins of Our Times* (London: Verso, 1994).

7   Michel Callon, "Introduction: The Embeddedness of Economic Markets in Economics," in *The Laws of the Markets,* ed. Michael Callon (Oxford: Blackwell Publishers, 1998), 1–57.

8   Ho, *Liquidated,* 36.

MODULE 4
THE AUTHOR'S CONTRIBUTION

KEY POINTS

- Ho's *Liquidated* challenges the popular understanding of financial crises as inevitable stages in market cycles, and exposes the Wall Street culture of liquidity* as a cause of economic instability.

- Ho takes an ethnographic* approach to prove her thesis, using interviews and participant observation* in investment banks,* and interpreting Wall Street in terms of its myths, rituals, and beliefs. In the course of "participant observation," the observer takes part in the behavior or culture he or she is observing.

- *Liquidated* contributes to debates in economic anthropology* and social studies of financial capitalism,* and to current understandings of financial crises in mainstream public discourse.* "Discourse" here refers to the system of language and assumptions we draw on when we discuss a subject.

Author's Aims

In *Liquidated: An Ethnography of Wall Street,* Karen Z. Ho aimed to demystify the world of finance, to "unpack markets ethnographically from the ground up, and in so doing, counter social-scientific tendencies to approach markets as undecipherable, abstract, totalizing, and all-powerful."[1] Ho tried to illustrate how the Wall Street culture of liquidity shapes the strategies of investment bankers in the financial market, which in turn influences American society and the global economy.

Ho intends to reveal what she sees as a reality too often masked by triumphalist interpretations of capitalist globalization*—

> 66 Because Wall Street investment bankers are highly visible in terms of their own self-representations and claims to truth and authority, yet culturally invisible in terms of their everyday practices and assumptions, by directly accessing key agents of change on Wall Street, a site widely deemed the epitome of global capitalist markets, I attempt to localize the very actors and institutions with a world-making influence on the global economy, and thus on the livelihoods of many. 99
>
> Karen Z. Ho, *Liquidated: An Ethnography of Wall Street*

interpretations of the global spread of the economic and social system of capitalism as some sort of moral victory—in order to allow society to tackle, once and for all, the socioeconomic inequalities produced and entrenched by the culture of liquidity.

Her aim is not only to illustrate how this particular culture is produced, but also to expose the reasons why Wall Streeters are culturally predisposed *against* pursuing the common good. Investment bankers and bank executives knowingly take risky decisions because they *cannot* be concerned with layoffs or long-term corporate development. This is due to their having gone through a process of acculturation*—they have acquired a set of beliefs and standards through exposure to others that hold them—in which they have acquired the culture of the investment bank and been separated from the lives of the nonelite.

While solutions to the problems that the culture of Wall Street causes are not directly asserted in Ho's writing, they are implicit in her argument. For example, as part of her interpretation of the history of shareholder value* as a central motivation of strategy in the finance sector, she writes that "[only] twenty-five years go, the public corporation in the United States was mainly viewed as a stable social institution ... judged according to a longer-term time frame that went beyond Wall Street's short term financial expectations."[2] The solution that follows from this observation is a divorce between the quarterly objectives of Wall Street investment banks and the long-term interests of public corporations.

Approach

Ho applies ethnographic thinking to consider the counterintuitive link between downsizing* and shareholder value. Anthropologists have traditionally conducted fieldwork in distant societies—distant in both cultural and geographic terms. Choosing Wall Street as a field site and looking at liquidity as if it were a distant culture is part of a more contemporary anthropological practice. By thinking more flexibly about notions of distance, Ho was able to observe both the physical segregation that results from the layouts used in the buildings that house financial institutions, and the discernible aura surrounding elite groups of investment bankers—often referred to as a "tribe."

In Wall Street, Ho conducted hundreds of interviews with employees to analyze their lives, daily routines, and workspaces. Importantly, she attempted to get an insider perspective by actually working in a financial institution. Her perspective is inherently anthropological because she looks at "Wall Street [histories] of shareholder entitlement and Wall Street's conception of itself as fundraiser to the world as origin myths," studying the practices in the financial sector as "indicative of a particular world view and socioeconomic interest rather than objective statements of fact."[3] To explain her reasons for taking this approach, she writes that by "delving into the narratives of capitalist mythmaking and their concurrent shaping of capitalist practices, I denaturalize the building blocks of shareholder value."[4] Her project, in other words, is to demonstrate that certain basic capitalist principles shared by those who work on Wall Street are more a question of myth than the expression of some "natural law."

Ho's long-term immersion in Wall Street investment banking, and engagement with the "native" point of view, results in a nuanced description of Wall Streeters' everyday life. At the same time, she is able to connect her on-the-ground perspective on investment banking with the intricacies of corporate America* and global finance. In this way she answers her core questions by approaching "the daily practices and corporate cultural values of investment bankers in the workplace as the site which links the cultural frame, dispositions, and habitus* of investment bankers with broader US corporate restructuring and the construction of financial market booms and busts."[5] "Habitus" is a term signifying the personality resulting from the specific social and cultural context that shaped it.

Contribution in Context

In the context of contemporary debates in economic anthropology and social studies of financial capitalism, *Liquidated* offers two main contributions. First, Ho disrupts the dominant, abstract idea of financial capitalism as regulated by mysterious and seemingly natural market rules. Second, in showing the cultural uniqueness of the logic underpinning the strategies of financial bankers, she offers a series of interpretive tools to understand the real causes of contemporary financial crises and the socioeconomic inequalities they cause.

Published at a time when the shock of the financial crisis of 2007–8 was reverberating through the lives of countless ordinary people around the world, *Liquidated* shows that financial crises are not the inevitable result of inbuilt structures of financial markets. For Ho, the dominant "construction of booms and busts are simply conflated with 'the market'" when they are actually the outcomes of strategies authored by living human beings, socialized by "particular work-place models, corporate culture, and organizational values of Wall Street financial institutions"[6] which encourages them to orchestrate financial collapses. These conclusions are relevant well beyond academia. As the

Financial Times journalist Gillian Tett* wrote: "[Ho's] insights are highly pertinent to the [financial crisis] of 2008, since this ethnography provides a wider cultural context and analysis than most journalistic books."[7]

NOTES

1   Karen Z. Ho, *Liquidated: An Ethnography of Wall Street* (Durham: Duke University Press, 2009), xi.

2   Ho, *Liquidated*, 3.

3   Ho, *Liquidated*, 29.

4   Ho, *Liquidated*, 171.

5   Ho, *Liquidated*, 4.

6   Ho, *Liquidated*, 11.

7   Gillian Tett, "Books of the Year: Gems among a string of credit-crunch tomes," *Management Today,* December 1, 2009, accessed October 9, 2015, http://www.managementtoday.co.uk/news/969289/Books-Year-Gems-among-string-credit-crunch-tomes/?DCMP=ILC-SEARCH.

SECTION 2
IDEAS

MODULE 5
MAIN IDEAS

KEY POINTS

- The main idea that Ho advances in *Liquidated* is that the causes of financial crises can be found in the practices of investment bankers,* encouraged by the culture of liquidity.*

- The culture of liquidity shapes not only the investment strategy of Wall Street,* but also the time frames, disciplines, and notions of efficiency of contemporary American corporations.

- Ho uses a narrative, mostly biographical, style to make the book more readable and accessible to non-specialists. She also uses full quotes from her interviews to illustrate difficult concepts in simple words.

Key Themes

In *Liquidated: An Ethnography of Wall Street*, Karen Z. Ho argues that Wall Street's culture of liquidity encourages financial bankers to make everything as liquid as possible—that is, easily bought, sold, or traded. This ideal of liquidity is applied to everything from financial to human capital, and even bankers' own personal and professional lives. Making everything as liquid as possible means turning "everything tangible … into liquid assets—sliced, diced and homogenized into negotiable commodities,"[1] accelerating their circulation and increasing the benefits without raising the costs. Ho demonstrates that this particular culture is socially constructed as a habitus,* or personal viewpoint absorbed through a broader culture—in the context of Wall Street, recruitment rituals, workplace conditions, and a value system based on shareholder value.*

Wall Street investment bankers recruit their workforce largely from

❝ Investment bankers' approaches to downsizing
and the financial markets are inseparable from the
structures and strategies of their own workplaces.
Their generalized understandings and daily practices
that shape the financial markets are framed through
their own experiences of compensation, job insecurity,
corporate restructuring, market identification, hard
work, and pinnacle status, and this employment habitus
in turn shapes (and is shaped by) how they approach
corporate America and how they influence the capital
markets and financial crises. ❞

Karen Z. Ho, *Liquidated: An Ethnography of Wall Street*

prestigious ("Ivy League") universities, where a culture of excellence
and privilege is already ingrained. They reinforce the students' self-image
as "the best and brightest" by engaging in a series of rituals during the
academic year, including dinners in expensive restaurants, social events in
luxurious exclusive settings, and spectacular recruitment presentations.
In this process, the students' academic achievements matter less than the
educational pedigree they possess as graduates of prestigious seats of
learning, and their motivation to make a lot of money.

Once hired, many of these new recruits find themselves working
as many as 100 hours per week. In addition, they know they will most
likely be downsized* as part of corporate restructuring. Still, most
new employees assert that long hours and job insecurity build
character, that their salary is proportionate to their commitment, and
their generous bonuses reflect their ability to close deals. These
grueling conditions tied to great earning prospects and the possibility
of fast money through bonuses, contribute to instilling the culture of
liquidity while justifying it with monetary meritocracy*—the idea
that the hardest workers will be the biggest earners.

Another justification for this culture of liquidity is the myth that maximizing shareholder value is the best way to serve stockowners and companies. Bankers insist that painful practices such as downsizing are done in the interest of shareholders, who are the actual owners of the company. However, using strategies such as merging, acquiring, laying off workers, and selling off units increase shareholder value only in the short term. While investment bankers increase their bonuses with each financial deal they complete, the momentary growth in the stock prices creates the impression of corporate efficiency. But it is only an illusion.

Exploring the Ideas

Ho argues that the culture of liquidity that is socially constructed by investment bankers is not limited to the financial sector. Rather, "the values and practices that have historically governed the stock market have been translated and utilized to govern corporations themselves."[2] This can be observed in the time frames, disciplines, and notions of efficiency of contemporary American corporations that have their origins in the stock market.

Referencing the "temporalities"—the way that time is organized—defining work in the financial sector, Ho writes: "Wall Street investment banks use stock-market temporalities* to frame and discipline the timeframes of corporations. Quarterly deadlines are ill-suited, not to mention detrimental, to long-range plans (such as research and development) that may not post rising profits each and every quarter, yet businesses are punished for not continually meeting these expectations."[3] In contrast, investment bankers are prized for their short-term growth of stock prices, regardless of the long-term effects.

Ho further argues that the idea of efficiency now refers to "the set of practices which most quickly and cheaply translates corporate actions into rising stock prices," and is measured "by the number and size of deals and transactions that create short-term stock price increases." In contrast, notions of efficiency as "grounded in labor and industrial productivity linked to sustained corporate growth are no longer appropriate"[4] to the contemporary American corporation.

Ho admits, however, that financial practices are not entirely disconnected from productive labor, as "financial transactions still necessitate a particular kind of labor from Wall Street, which in turn depends on the accumulated surplus value from labor in corporate assets."[5] Nevertheless, it is because of the increasing separation from productive labor that American corporations have been restructured according to the agendas of Wall Street.

Language and Expression

Ho wrote *Liquidated* as an ethnography,* portraying herself as an anthropologist and graduate student immersed in a strange culture. She deals with complex issues in the fields of financial banking, corporate management, and stock market exchange. As such, this project requires the manipulation of a sometimes dizzying collection of both social-scientific language and specialist jargon from the world of finance. In order to help the reader navigate the text, she often introduces and explains these terms. For example, she writes: "Junk bonds* are, in essence, risky bonds: they offer the holder of the bond (the lender of money) the enticement of extremely high returns, but the flipside is that they are very risky and could become worthless at any time."[6]

Sometimes, she uses direct quotations from her interviews to explain, in accessible language, processes that might sound unfamiliar to the nonspecialist reader. At one point, for example, she hands the narration over to her informant (an individual supplying information as part of an ethnographic study), quoting him at length to illustrate the takeover process: "What they [private equity firms] do is they will use the high yield we raise [the junk bonds that the bank helps them to issue], put in a little bit of money themselves, buy a company, use the company's cash flow to pay down the debt … So that their pie, which was really small, just keeps growing as the company pays down the debt. So that when they sell the company—three or five years later … by that time the debt is a much lower percentage of the overall value of the company and the value of their equity is much higher, and those guys will make a fortune, an absolute fortune."[7]

Ho uses a narrative style to place these complex issues and often confusing terminology in the story of her own journey into the world of finance, and the stories of the people she encounters there. She begins the book with a biographical tone—"I first became interested in studying Wall Street on 21 September 1995"[8]—and repeatedly uses these storytelling techniques throughout the book, which at times reads like a novel. As the anthropologist Keith Hart* observed: "What holds the book together is a story that is both world-historical and personal."[9]

NOTES

1   "Nonfiction Book Review: *Liquidated: An Ethnography of Wall Street* by Karen Zouwen Ho," PublishersWeekly.com, accessed October 10, 2015, http://www.publishersweekly.com/978-0-8223-4599-2.

2   Karen Z. Ho, *Liquidated: An Ethnography of Wall Street* (Durham: Duke University Press, 2009), 167.

3   Ho, *Liquidated*, 165.

4   Ho, *Liquidated*, 163.

5   Ho, *Liquidated*, 163.

6   Ho, *Liquidated*, 142.

7   Ho, *Liquidated*, 143.

8   Ho, *Liquidated*, 1.

9   Keith Hart, "Review of *Liquidated: An Ethnography of Wall Street* by Karen Ho," *American Ethnologist* 38, no. 2 (2011): 379.

MODULE 6
SECONDARY IDEAS

KEY POINTS

- In *Liquidated*, Karen Ho illustrates that increasing shareholder value* is Wall Street's* principal goal, even though it does not necessarily equate with the financial health of a company or its stocks.

- Shareholder value has become top priority in Wall Street because it justified the shareholder revolution* (a period in the 1980s when investment banks* started to take over companies with the purpose of breaking them up and selling them on the financial market) and because it became a symbol of the "natural" state of the economy.

- Even though Ho was trying to raise public awareness of the fundamental causes of financial crises, her attempt to make the book accessible to a wide audience has generally been overlooked.

Other Ideas

In *Liquidated: An Ethnography of Wall Street*, Karen Z. Ho argues that shareholder value is the most important concept with which Wall Streeters make "sense of the world and their place in it: it shaped how they used their 'smartness' and explained the purpose of their hard work."[1] This concept permeates the discourses* of investment bankers, research analysts, traders, and stock managers. For them, creating shareholder value means more than "raising the stock price of a corporation: it also signified a mission statement, a declaration of purpose, even a call to action. Creating or reclaiming shareholder value was morally and economically the right thing to do; it was the yardstick to measure individual as well as corporate practices, values, and achievements."[2]

> ❝ Take Morgan [Stanley investment firm], for example. We have long been accused of having too much fat. We have gone through a process of kind of trimming people out. And the day it was announced we would be trimming our workforce, our stock price jumped three bucks because people recognized that we were finally getting down to trying to become a lean, mean investment bank... ❞
>
> Karen Z. Ho, *Liquidated: An Ethnography of Wall Street*

Wall Streeters create shareholder value through a set of financial and managerial measures, such as laying off parts of a workforce. It might sound counterintuitive to relate laying off to increasing shareholder value; from a commonsense point of view, downsizing* should be a signal of poor financial health.

However, from an insider point of view, it makes sense. As soon as a corporation announces its intention to downsize, the financial market interprets that decision as an indicator of the company's first step to increasing efficiency. By cutting costs such as employees' salaries, pensions, and insurance costs, the company implicitly promises to get into financial health very soon, and it is this "promise" of improvement that causes the price to increase. As one of the people Ho interviewed in the course of her study tells us: "The market is looking for you to act. It is going to mean laying off workforce and taking a big restructuring charge to become the entity you said you were going to become."[3]

Exploring the Ideas

Even though Wall Streeters hold shareholder value as paramount, they are simultaneously aware that the supposed link between persistently rising stock prices and downsizings often breaks down as a result of bad bets and poor strategies[4] such as the subprime mortgage debacle,* the junk bond crisis,* and Black Monday* (various financial crises that arose from the culture of the US financial sector). This is one of the paradoxes Ho is determined to understand, asking her Wall Street informants why they insist on structuring their value system and their work practices in a way that repeatedly causes negative returns.

One answer she finds is historical. Initially, shareholder value became important because it justified the takeover movement. In the 1980s, it became common for many skillful traders to buy a company on the stock market with money obtained by selling high-yield bonds to future shareholders. Then, they would downsize and restructure the company in order to pay off the debt, and eventually sell the company to make a profit.

"Although the act of liquidating a corporation to pay off private debt was viewed as destructive and even revolting by critics and the mainstream corporate community alike, dissent was often muted because raiders and bankers were able to link their activities to the necessary pains of shareholder revolution."[5]

In other words, they made such practice socially acceptable; by earning interest for their shareholders, they introduced the idea that buying and breaking up a company is a viable way to create value.

However, Wall Streeters' current understanding of shareholder value "rests not only on a crude reinterpretation of the historical relationships between corporate America,* the stock market, and investors, but also on decontextualized extrapolations (and new adaptations) from neoclassical* and classical* economic thought."[6] In other words, Wall Streeters hold up shareholder value as the supreme concept in the "natural" state of economic life, and have found ways to justify this belief. By turning everything into a commodity and decreasing the time it takes to exchange it, they realize the extreme model of liquidity.* Eventually, they project this ultimate conception of liquidity on to the American economy as a whole.

For key players in the finance sector, liquidity equates with efficiency and should have positive consequences on the economy because it forces companies to become more responsive to market changes. However, since bankers equate efficiency with risky choices too, regardless of the negative social consequences, their obsession with liquidity eventually becomes a repeated cause of economic crises.

Overlooked

Reviewers, critics, and colleagues in economic anthropology* and the anthropology* of finance received *Liquidated* with enthusiasm. They particularly praised Ho's methodology, theoretical argument, and data collection. Less attention, however, has been paid to the work's social impact.

Ho wanted the message of the book to reach beyond academic circles. Indeed, she writes that an "intellectual commitment to social and economic justice first galvanized this book's journey."[7] However, Ho's attempt to make the book accessible to a wide audience has been generally overlooked. Ho uses a series of writing strategies that clearly indicate that she was trying to raise public awareness of rather specialist and obscure phenomena, such as shareholder value and liquid habitus* (a word designating the role that a specific social and cultural context plays in shaping the personality of those immersed in it).

One of the rhetorical strategies she uses corresponds to what the anthropologist Thomas H. Eriksen* has called "the Riddle"[8]—an approach to writing about anthropology using specific narrative techniques to make it more accessible. Ho begins the book with a puzzling question and takes a retrospective narrative tone to answer it. She looks back at the memories from her first Wall Street job, her friends and colleagues, so that her inductive reasoning* (statements that link evidence and conclusion) merges with her biography. There is, indeed, an echo of detective fiction underlying the narrative, using suspense to compel the reader to find out who is ultimately responsible for current financial crises.

Even though this and other narrative strategies were intended to improve the reading experience, this aspect of Ho's work has not been recognized. In a review of *Liquidated*, the University of Georgia scholar Alexandra B. Cox flatly rules Ho's writing as unsuitable for a general audience: "The sentence structure, word choice, and overall readability are challenging and more appropriate for an academic audience. The text was adapted from her dissertation, and it remains perhaps too scholarly for popular consumption."[9]

The fact that her attempt to reach a wider public was not recognized seems to indicate that she has not fully succeeded in explaining Wall Street's culture of liquidity in the manner she intended.

NOTES

1   Karen Ho, *Liquidated: An Ethnography of Wall Street* (Durham: Duke University Press, 2009), 123.

2   Ho, *Liquidated,* 125.

3   Ho, *Liquidated,* 161.

4   Ho, *Liquidated,* 168.

5   Ho, *Liquidated,* 142.

6   Ho, *Liquidated,* 169.

7   Ho, *Liquidated*, ix.

8   Thomas Hylland Eriksen, *Engaging Anthropology: The Case for a Public Presence* (Oxford: Berg, 2006).

9   Alexandra B. Cox, "Making Markets and Constructing Crises: A Review of Ho's *Liquidated*," *The Qualitative Report* 17 (2012): 4.

MODULE 7
ACHIEVEMENT

KEY POINTS

- Karen Z. Ho has succeeded in using the concept of habitus*—the idea that the personality of an individual is defined by the particular social or cultural context in which they are immersed—to illustrate the link between shareholder value,* the practices of Wall Streeters,* and financial crises.

- While Ho has shown that ethnographic* methods can provide a unique perspective from which to look at Wall Street, critics point out that her historical discussion does not add much to the existing literature.

- Ho's connection between the habitus of bankers and the changing face of corporate America* is much stronger than the link she draws between the culture of Wall Street and its global consequences.

Assessing the Argument

In *Liquidated: An Ethnography of Wall Street*, Karen Z. Ho argues that the myths, rituals, and world view of Wall Street investment bankers* construct a culture of liquidity* that causes both financial crises and the reshaping of corporate America. Wall Street bankers are culturally predisposed to implement risky financial strategies, supposedly for the sake of raising the price of their stocks. Wall Street practices aimed at generating short-term gains have transformed American corporations from production- and development-oriented enterprises into mere means of increasing shareholder value.

While financial crashes are often perceived as "natural" events in market cycles, *Liquidated* illustrates the concrete link connecting Wall

> ❝ My analysis of Wall Street's shareholder value worldviews has shown that the values and practices that have historically governed the stock market have been translated and utilized to govern corporations themselves. ❞
>
> Karen Z. Ho, *Liquidated: An Ethnography of Wall Street*

Street culture with the habitus of investment bankers. The book demonstrates, then, that financial breakdowns are more a question of the social landscape that defines Wall Street rather than "natural," inbuilt, features of the market. Ho successfully achieves her aims by organizing her material as an inductive analysis: it proceeds, that is, from a clearly stated question, to ethnographic description, analytical discussion, and a solid and convincing conclusion.

Ho uses specialist terms and ideas—centrally Pierre Bourdieu's* concept of habitus—to weave ethnographic observation and a theoretical argument about corporate America and financial crises into a narrative of her experience on Wall Street. Her description of recruitment rituals illustrates how the self-image of being "the best and the brightest" is consolidated into future employees at the earliest possible point. Detailed observations of the daily lives of those working on Wall Street expose their high-pressured and precarious working conditions where risky strategies designed to yield short-term gains are generously rewarded. In these conditions they develop the habitus of liquidity.

Ho goes on to connect her observations of her subjects with American economic history by showing how the lives of those who work on Wall Street are part of a larger historical process, which marked the shaping of corporate America in the image of investment bankers. Finally, in a solid example of inductive reasoning* she connects these cultural predispositions and historical processes to the general instability of the financial market.

Achievement in Context

Using ethnography* to study a segment of a dominant Western culture is a definitive break with the traditions of anthropological practice. As Ho mentions in the book's acknowledgements, while "centers of power within the United States [were] still uncharted territory for most anthropologists" her "search to understand the massive sea changes occurring in American business practices during the past three decades took [her] to the doorstep of Wall Street investment banks, an unconventional site for anthropological research."[1]

Liquidated enjoyed a warm reception from the subfield of economic anthropology* in particular. In his review, Giuseppe Caruso of the University of Helsinki wrote: "Ho's groundbreaking work succeeds in providing the reader with a convincing argument that the anthropology* of capitalism* is not impervious to small scale ethnography which instead gives abstract capitalism a grounded dimension, showing its instantiation in daily practices, ideologies and institutions," and calls her book, "a milestone of an increasingly sophisticated and relevant anthropology of markets."[2] The anthropologist of money Keith Hart* enthusiastically welcomed the book in his review, writing: "Ho has provided a canonical text for our era. She set out to do it from the start and she has succeeded. The rest of us can now chew over its significance for our own work."[3]

In the context of historical studies of finance, Ho's contribution is not necessarily groundbreaking. Her historical discussion of the influence of investment banking on American corporations in the 1980s and 1990s provides important background information to contextualize her findings, but does not add anything new to the existing body of literature on the subject.[4] Given that Ho's intention was to provide a novel ethnography and not to innovate the historical understanding of financial markets, this is hardly surprising.

Limitations

In *Liquidated*, Ho establishes an evidence-based correlation between the culture of Wall Street and the American financial market, but the link between Wall Street and the global financial markets is relatively less developed. However, this specific limitation is actually a general anthropological affliction in the study of finance. For instance, the British anthropologist Keith Hart observed that since the 1980s "anthropologists [of money and finance] have found it hard to link their detailed ethnographic accounts to world history in the longer run."[5]

Some of the later chapters in *Liquidated* might betray a certain lack of confidence in the author's ability to demonstrate in concrete terms the connection between, as she puts it, "the mutual constitution of the local and the global—the specific techniques, social ramifications, and self-effects of American bankers' promotion of globalization* and claiming of the whole world."[6] Rather than illustrating investment bankers' global influence, parts of the book are better equipped to demonstrate bankers' *belief* in their pervasive global presence (through, for example, their use of "global talk"—reference to the global reach of their institutions—in order to exaggerate their omnipresence and convince investors to buy their stocks). It follows that, arguably, Ho has not necessarily achieved her stated aim of connecting the culture of liquidity of Wall Street with its global effects.

While *Liquidated* is firmly grounded in insights derived from interviews with junior and senior traders, research analysts, management consultants, and emerging market experts, less material is presented from the CEOs, top executives, and top managers of investment banks. Given that one of her aims was to counterbalance popular understandings of financial capitalism as a mere result of top-down implementations of supposedly impersonal laws of the market, a description of how investment banks' most powerful players contribute to creating and maintaining Wall Street culture might have strengthened Ho's project.

NOTES

1   Karen Ho, *Liquidated: An Ethnography of Wall Street* (Durham: Duke University Press, 2009), ix.

2   Giuseppe Caruso, "*Liquidated. An Ethnography of Wall Street* by Karen Ho," *The Experience of Collective Action,* May 17, 2011, accessed October 11, 2015, https://giuseppecaruso.wordpress.com/2011/05/17/liquidated-an-ethnography-of-wall-street-by-karen-ho/.

3   Keith Hart, "Review of *Liquidated: An Ethnography of Wall Street* by Karen Ho," *American Ethnologist* 38, no. 2 (May 1, 2011): 378.

4   Mansel G. Blackford, "*Liquidated: An Ethnography of Wall Street*," *The Business History Review* 85, no. 3 (2011): 628.

5   Keith Hart and Horacio Ortiz, "The Anthropology of Money and Finance: Between Ethnography and World History," *Annual Review of Anthropology* 43 (2014): 467.

6   Ho, *Liquidated*, 296.

MODULE 8
PLACE IN THE AUTHOR'S WORK

KEY POINTS

- Ho published *Liquidated* about a decade after her doctoral studies. Her earlier publications anticipated some of the material of this book and some preliminary formulations of her main arguments.

- During a long career, Parker has returned time and again to explaining the dramatic events of the sixteenth and seventeenth centuries, especially in Europe.

- *Global Crisis* was published amid an increasingly urgent worldwide debate about climate change and offered the possibility that lessons from the past might help make policy for the future.

Positioning

Liquidated: An Ethnography of Wall Street was published in 2009, roughly ten years after Karen Ho completed her PhD. Her earlier articles from that decade anticipated the material in the book and contained preliminary formulations of her main arguments.

She published one such article in 2005, the paper "Situating Global Capitalisms."[1] The article illustrates that Wall Street's* global presence is often only for show, citing as evidence examples like empty or understaffed offices in a foreign country to increase the perceived value of stocks. Ho's argument was intended to show that the popular impression of "global" presence is sometimes based on flimsy assumptions, which collapse under closer scrutiny. Along with this theoretical point, in "Situating Global Capitalisms" Ho presented some of her initial reflections on her ethnographic*material, including her experience of recruitment events at Princeton University, orientation

> **❝** The intelligence of its author shines through *Liquidated*. It is, like any first book, work in progress, but work at a consistently high level and the writing is robust enough to match Ho's intellectual ambition. I found it rewarding to read and reflect on, a landmark in the burgeoning anthropology of money. **❞**
>
> Keith Hart, "Review of *Liquidated*"

sessions at an investment bank,* and a number of fragments from her hundreds of interviews with workers in the finance sector.

In a second article, published a few months before *Liquidated*, "Disciplining Investment Bankers, Disciplining the Economy,"[2] Ho analyses "two pivotal socioeconomic phenomena—rampant downsizings* throughout 'corporate America'* and the financial bubble and bust of 2001."[3] In it, Ho uses investment bankers' own perspectives to illustrate the rationale behind corporate downsizing. Her point is, once again, that financial capitalism* is too often understood as abstract and separated from social and cultural reality. Ho sets herself the task of revealing how financial markets are grounded in the everyday practices and beliefs of the people who work on Wall Street. To do so, she anticipates some of the ethnographic material of her forthcoming book, including bankers' central beliefs, interviews with financial analysts and managers, and the incompatibility between Wall Street quarterly expectations and corporate long-term time schemes.

Integration

Ho's publications reveal her longstanding engagement with the issues that can be found throughout *Liquidated*. In "Situating Global Capitalisms" (2005), for example, Ho was already opposing abstract ideas about capitalism with her bottom–up perspective, asking: "To what extent do critical theorists, despite their professed awareness of the contingencies, constructed effects, and productive strategies of global capitalism, take capitalist pronouncements at face value,"[4] instead of critically dissecting their cultural practices? Questioning what other theorists have taken for granted, or considered "natural" or inevitable, is a longstanding hallmark of Ho's approach.

With *Liquidated*, she advances her criticisms of these misguided perceptions with a well-structured analytical progression from data gathered in the field to a sophisticated theoretical argument.

Similarly, in her 2009 article "Disciplining Investment Bankers, Disciplining the Economy," Ho presented her ethnographic study of Wall Street "to counter anthropological approaches to money and finance as 'abstract.'"[5] Again, she demonstrates that Wall Street culture of liquidity* is the root cause of financial crises and corporate downsizing, thereby challenging widespread understandings of such phenomena as inevitable consequences of market cycles and financial structures.

Significance

Ho's aim to spread a more concrete conception of finance and capitalism situates her work within the substantivist* tradition. Substantivist anthropologists such as Karl P. Polanyi,* Marshall Sahlins,* and Stephen Gudeman,* insisted that the formalist* position on the economy—that neoclassical* abstract economic models are universally applicable—is simply wrong. Instead, they work to establish concrete connections between each particular culture and its economy.

Even though the substantivist position has generally been applied in the field of economic anthropology,* Karen Ho argued that some anthropologists of finance still rather rely on *models* to represent economic reality where *description* would generate a clearer picture.[6] Following this logic, Ho's research draws on the everyday lives and working practices of real people to show how the Wall Street culture of liquidity is created and maintained.

Such original, long-term, in-depth engagement has earned Ho widespread popularity and academic recognition. Since the publication of *Liquidated*, she has been the lead author for the "Finance" entry in the *Encyclopedia of Social and Cultural Anthropology,* a role that confirms her position as a leading authority on the subject.[7] Reviews of *Liquidated* were almost unanimously positive, and many of the leading thinkers in her field have expressed their belief that the book will become a seminal text.

NOTES

1   Karen Z. Ho, "Situating Global Capitalisms: A View from Wall Street Investment Banks," *Cultural Anthropology* 20, no. 1 (2005): 68–96.

2   Karen Z. Ho, "Disciplining Investment Bankers, Disciplining the Economy: Wall Street's Institutional Culture of Crisis and the Downsizing of 'Corporate America'," *American Anthropologist* 111, no. 2 (2009): 177–89.

3   Ho, "Disciplining Investment Bankers, Disciplining the Economy," 177.

4   Ho, "Situating Global Capitalisms," 68.

5   Ho, "Disciplining Investment Bankers, Disciplining the Economy," 187.

6   Karen Z. Ho, *Liquidated: An Ethnography of Wall Street* (Durham: Duke University Press, 2009), 34–38; see also, Karen Z. Ho, "Commentary on Andrew Orta's 'Managing the Margins': The Anthropology of Transnational Capitalism, Neoliberalism, and Risk," *American Ethnologist* 41, no. 1 (February 1, 2014): 33.

7   Karen Z. Ho, "Finance," in *Encyclopedia of Social and Cultural Anthropology, 2nd Ed.,* eds Alan Barnard and Jonathan Spencer, (London and New York: Routledge, 2010), 295–8.

SECTION 3
IMPACT

MODULE 9
THE FIRST RESPONSES

KEY POINTS

- While Karen Z. Ho's *Liquidated* was widely praised for the accuracy of her ethnographic* method, her critics argued her history of Wall Street* and its connection to global finance was less compelling.

- Ho drew on the criticism concerning the lack of perspective from top executives in *Liquidated* in the continuation of her research.

- There is a consensus among scholars about the substantial contribution of *Liquidated* to the field of economic anthropology* in general and anthropology* of finance in particular.

Criticism

When Karen Z. Ho published *Liquidated: An Ethnography of Wall Street*, the book was widely praised in the international anthropological community and beyond. She has been commended for her sharp attention to the details of Wall Streeters' process of acculturation* (the process through which a person acquires the culture of a different group through spending time with its members), her accurate and sensitive descriptions of their daily routines and work environment, and her keen observation of the intricate connections between these lived experiences and their ideological and cultural counterparts.[1] Some, however, felt that Ho did not necessarily elaborate other aspects of her research, such as the emergence of the shareholder value* movement in the 1980s (the practice of buying companies for the sole purpose of restructuring and reselling the parts at a higher value) with the same depth of attention.

> **❝** Karen Ho is my hero ... Her ethnography of
> investment bankers in the late 1990s, *Liquidated*, depicts
> the bravado, callousness, and contradictions that are the
> hallmarks of investment banking culture. **❞**
>
> Mitchel Y. Abolafia, "*Liquidated*," review for the *American Journal of Sociology*

The changing relationship between American corporations and investment banking*has been the subject of a vast body of literature in both history and business studies. Even in his positive review of *Liquidated*, the social scientist Mitchel Abolafia* highlighted this weak spot in the book, noting: "Ho's treatment of the shareholder value movement would have benefited from a greater familiarity with the literature on the corporation and corporate finance in organization theory."[2] Professor Mansel Blackford believes that, as a consequence, Ho's "critical point ... that investment bankers from the 1980s on misread history ... has little basis in the historical record. Circumstances were never that simple, for corporate managers had diverse objectives."[3] In summary, as the anthropologist Keith Hart* put it, "once we have finished congratulating Ho on taking the ethnographic method to Wall Street, there are other questions to be answered concerning comparative history and various bodies of theoretical literature."[4]

Another aspect that Ho's research overlooked is the way in which the culture of Wall Street is regarded and constructed by top executives. Presumably, this is a result of her limited access to the top floors of the investment banks. Her informants are mostly students, early-career employees, junior and senior investment bankers.

Responses

Karen Ho did not respond directly to the criticisms to *Liquidated*. Since the reaction to the publication was mostly positive, criticisms were rare and not particularly severe, generally providing a sense of balance and scholarly consideration. *Liquidated* does not present a revolutionary new theory, but rather an application of earlier culturalist perspectives on the economy, one that is largely accepted in the anthropological community. Criticisms leveled against the work generally addressed marginal aspects of Ho's argument rather than central elements.

Ho has not ignored her critics. It appears that she has welcomed the criticism concerning the lack of top executive perspectives in *Liquidated*, and used this point to direct her ongoing research. In her 2014 article "Commentary on Andrew Orta's* 'Managing the Margins'" she wrote that her "current informants" (suppliers of ethnographic data from the inside) include "retired corporate executives and managers (who used to work in bureaucratic organizations that are now actively financialized)."[5] Although the insights from this research are yet to be published, it is reasonable to expect that the perspectives of these powerful players will expand the argument presented in *Liquidated*.

Conflict and Consensus

In the field of economic anthropology in general, and the subfield of anthropology of finance in particular, there is a solid consensus that *Liquidated* has made a substantial, positive contribution. Ho's peers recognize her convincing and creative use of substantivist* theory and method in an area few anthropologists had approached in such depth. Since most—if not all—economic anthropologists identify with the substantivist tradition, an application of its principles to the issue of Wall Street financial capitalism* could only be welcomed warmly.

Ho drew on the substantivist position that economy is not a singular mass of supposedly natural, universal economic principles. She looks at economies in the plural, and in particular at the culture that produces the specific formulation of the contemporary Wall Street financial market. However, Ho does not necessarily aim to reproduce "the native point of view," as ethnographers customarily do. Keith Hart takes up this point, noting: "This book is striking for its refusal to stick with the local actors' point of view, as most previous ethnographies of financial activities have."[6]

Indeed, a key part of Ho's method involves challenging the popular view of market capitalism, and its consequences, as natural and inevitable; reproducing the perspective of her informants too closely would amount to exactly that. As she wrote in 2014: "Careful attention is required, in ethnographic [studies of finance], not to reinscribe dominant assumptions of what constitutes capitalist motivations and approaches to risk, not to mention, the very context of capitalism itself."[7] That has arguably become the core of the continuing debate around *Liquidated*: its value, uses, and problems.

NOTES

1 Alexandra B. Cox, "Making Markets and Constructing Crises: A Review of Ho's *Liquidated*," *The Qualitative Report* 17 (2012): 1–4; Mitchel Y. Abolafia, "*Liquidated: An Ethnography of Wall Street* by Karen Ho," *American Journal of Sociology* 116, no. 1 (2010): 272–3; Mansel G. Blackford, "*Liquidated: An Ethnography of Wall Street*," *The Business History Review* 85, no. 3 (2011): 627–9; Keith Hart, "Review of *Liquidated: An Ethnography of Wall Street* by Karen Ho," *American Ethnologist* 38, no. 2 (2011): 378–9.

2 Abolafia, "*Liquidated: An Ethnography of Wall Street* by Karen Ho," 273.

3 Blackford, "*Liquidated: An Ethnography of Wall Street*," 628.

4 Hart, "Review of *Liquidated: An Ethnography of Wall Street* by Karen Ho," 379.

5 Karen Z. Ho, "Commentary on Andrew Orta's 'Managing the Margins': The Anthropology of Transnational Capitalism, Neoliberalism, and Risk," *American Ethnologist* 41, no. 1 (2014): 31.

6 Hart, "Review of *Liquidated: An Ethnography of Wall Street* by Karen Ho," 379.

7 Ho, "Commentary on Andrew Orta's 'Managing the Margins,' 31.

MODULE 10
THE EVOLVING DEBATE

KEY POINTS

- Ho's work makes a significant contribution to the contemporary debate about how to establish a theory and methodology in order to study global financial capitalism* in an ethnographic fashion.*

- *Liquidated* is not a foundational text of a school of thought but, rather, an expression of an existing school of thought—substantivism;* the book both consolidates and expands this position.

- Though Ho's ideas that finance should be studied on the basis of daily practices is not necessarily new, it is useful to remind economic anthropologists* of the risk of reproducing capitalist discourses.*

Uses and Problems

Among the many points that Karen Ho discusses in *Liquidated: An Ethnography of Wall Street*, authors currently involved in the debates about how to study global capitalism have taken up one in particular. Ho's work is regarded as genuinely engaging in the project of grounding global financial capitalism in the daily practices of real people, as opposed to simply being part of an ongoing theoretical debate. For example, the US ethnographer Stuart Alexander Rockefeller,* in a 2011 article about the uses of the term "flow" in capitalist discourse, cites Ho's argument to show how this idiom contributes to the widespread perception that capitalism is an immaterial force beyond the reach of human action[1]—something so natural, in other words, as to have "physical" properties.

The assumption that capitalism is inherently nonlocal and

> **"**... given the rise of neoliberalism and its resurgent representations of abstracting and globalizing markets, many scholars, especially when referring to Western money and finance, revert back to our legacy of binary assumptions where the financial dominance of investment banks are often attributed to abstract, all-powerful global markets. **"**
>
> Karen Z. Ho, *Liquidated: An Ethnography of Wall Street*

nonhuman involves bringing the capitalists' own self-perception into the theory. The point, in other words, is that ethnographers who do not critically examine capitalism's internal language—both formal and informal—risk reproducing its rhetoric in their own ethnographies, thereby justifying much of the capitalist status quo.

Ho engaged in an exchange of views on this issue with the anthropologist Andrew Orta.* Orta conducted his ethnographic research among business students on a short-term study-abroad course, which he interpreted as a context in which future executives and managers construct a transnational habitus* for business. In her commentary on the article, Ho noted that "too often, anthropologists take the rhetoric of capitalism and markets at face value and reproduce their self-representations as universal logics"—that is, in uncritically adopting the language used to discuss capitalism, they reaffirm its status as something universal. "Orta's large-scale narratives of broad capitalist change," she continues, "showcase the need to question our analytical domains and what we associate with them."[2]

Orta defends himself from the charge: "Acknowledging 'a broader world of business' need not mean taking the rhetorical self-representations of capitalism as universal truths. Indeed, I show that broader world to be itself subject to the representational and commensurating practices of [the] cultural production [typical of business courses]"[3]—that is (he argues), business students, and the courses they take, have a role in formulating and changing the ways in which capitalism is described and understood.

Right or wrong, these positions illustrate that Ho's work bears considerable relevance in the contemporary debate regarding the theory and methodology of studying global financial capitalism in an ethnographic manner.

Schools of Thought

Liquidated is unlikely to be considered the foundational text of a school of thought. Ho's contribution to the anthropological study of finance, though undeniably solid, is not necessarily revolutionary. Indeed, her ethnographic method and theoretical framework draws extensively on the long-established school of thought known as "economic substantivism."

Ho's contribution to the substantivist position comes from her convincing application of the ethnographic method to the context of Wall Street* investment banking.* In addition, her discussion of the link between certain socioeconomic assumptions and the culture of liquidity* makes a novel contribution to the anthropology of finance. As much as earlier thinkers were able to illustrate how the economy of, say, the indigenous hunter-gatherer populations of the Southern African Kalahari desert was substantially rooted in their specific culture, so Ho illustrates the deep entanglement of Wall Street investment banking in the culture of liquidity.

Liquidated is the recognizable product of an intellectual tradition in economic anthropology; it both confirms and expands this tradition. Ho adds fresh evidence that the substantivist position provides a valuable perspective from which to look at the financial economy of Wall Street; in turn, this has considerable implications for contemporary debates around the practices of Wall Street bankers. Most importantly, perhaps, it shows that ethnographic methods are not especially suited to the study of non-Western, nonmarket societies. On the contrary, they can shed new light on our understanding of Western financial institutions.

In Current Scholarship

Karen Ho's *Liquidated* is a recent contribution to its field, published in 2009. The idea that economic practices must be understood as taking place inside complex webs of social relations that "make markets" has been formulated, debated, and refined in previous studies by anthropologists such as Mitchel Abolafia,* Bill Maurer,* and Hirokazu Miyazaki.*

Ho observed that some scholars still tend to reproduce the world view, idioms, and concepts of capitalist* discourses,* rather than critically examining them. That, she argues, is mostly due to the enduring influence of neoliberalist* thought, according to which, global markets are understood as abstract (somehow immaterial), dominant, and all-encompassing.[4] She therefore builds on Maurer's idea that anthropologists of finance too often tend to reproduce the American economist Karl Polanyi's* scheme of "the great transformation," the evolutionary tale that sees economy as increasingly removed from society:"a linear trajectory from barter to metal coin, to paper backed by metal, to paper declared valuable by fiat, and finally, perhaps to complex financial entities like derivatives, with future, not anterior, backing."[5]

Karen Ho is not the first anthropologist to study financial instruments* (assets that can be traded to produce value) as a set of practices—social behaviors— embedded in a particular culture. Given the increasing relevance of financial institutions in contemporary global societies, however, and the growing interest in studying them in ethnographic terms, approaches such as Ho's that vigilantly guard against affirming dominant views of the economy as something abstract and somehow inevitable, given the nature of human economic behavior, are extremely important.

Arguing from a position formulated with a degree of critical rigor, there is no doubt *Liquidated* will continue to have considerable influence in the fields of economic anthropology and the anthropology of finance.

NOTES

1   Stuart A. Rockefeller, "'Flow,'" *Current Anthropology* 52, no. 4 (2011): 557–78.

2   Karen Z. Ho, "Commentary on Andrew Orta's 'Managing the Margins': The Anthropology of Transnational Capitalism, Neoliberalism, and Risk," *American Ethnologist* 41, no. 1 (2014), 33.

3   Andrew Orta, "Cultures of Capitalism, Contexts of Capitalism (Reply to Karen Ho)," *American Ethnologist* 41, no. 1 (2014), 39.

4   Karen Z. Ho, *Liquidated: An Ethnography of Wall Street* (Durham: Duke University Press, 2009), 32–3.

5   Bill Maurer, *Mutual Life, Limited: Islamic Banking, Alternative Currencies, Lateral Reason* (Princeton, NJ: Princeton University Press, 2005), 100.

MODULE 11
IMPACT AND INFLUENCE TODAY

KEY POINTS

- Even though Karen Z. Ho is not the only anthropologist who has written on finance, she has become one of the main references for the ethnographic* study of Wall Street.*

- *Liquidated* was welcomed as an original substantivist* ethnography in the growing field of anthropology* of finance, and as a clear-sighted study of the links between Wall Street's culture of liquidity* and financial crises.

- The book is inspiring a growing number of authors to advance new hypotheses, identify possible sites of research, and formulate new questions concerning the anthropological study of finance.

Position

It is fair to say that Karen Z. Ho's *Liquidated: An Ethnography of Wall Street* was a groundbreaking text; the financial journalist Gillian Tett* wrote that "[a] couple of decades ago it would have been quite hard to find anybody on Wall Street who claimed to be an anthropologist."[1] Ho was not only able to become an anthropologist of Wall Street, but also to convince many readers—both inside and outside anthropology—that ethnography* can tell us more about Wall Street than other approaches. In so doing, she has authoritatively positioned herself as the ethnographer who, by means of her focus on the lived experiences and culture of real people, reconciled "the mystique of finance" with the "mundane" (everyday).[2]

Karen Ho is by no means the only anthropologist who has written on Wall Street, however; as the economic anthropologist* Bill Maurer* noted: "In anthropology, it seems everyone has something to say about

> ❝ As I worked at a Wall Street investment bank in 1996–97 and then began intensive ethnographic fieldwork in 1998, shareholder value was just on the cusp of inundating American culture as the central explanation and rationale for corporate restructuring, changing concepts of wealth and inequality, and the state of the American economy. ❞
>
> Karen Z. Ho, *Liquidated: An Ethnography of Wall Street*

finance these days."[3] That is arguably because the abstract models of neoliberal* economics have become particularly unpopular in the aftermath of the 2007–8 financial crisis. In contrast, ethnographic approaches are gaining credibility. For example, Tett also wrote: "Anthropology can be extremely useful for understanding the contemporary financial world because of all the micro-level communities—or 'tribes' to use the cliché term—that are cropping up around the financial system."[4]

While Ho was not the first ethnographic researcher to approach Wall Street as the "new exotic,"[5] few anthropologists of finance have enjoyed as much attention and recognition. *Liquidated* has earned academic awards, including honorable mentions (in 2009 and 2010), and Ho has been an invited speaker on the popular American news and opinion television program *Up with Chris Hayes*.*[6] Anthropologists are seldom given such opportunities to influence public opinion, even though they usually deal with issues of deep public relevance. Arguably, Ho gained this attention because she was able to explain a complex matter that lay people were eager to understand but found hard to grasp because they lacked the necessary specialist financial knowledge.

Interaction

Liquidated was well-received both inside and outside academia. In academia, it was welcomed as an innovative ethnography in the growing field of anthropology of finance, a valuable contribution to the substantivist position, and a clear illustration of the methodological and theoretical potential of using ethnographic methods in Wall Street. It has already begun to serve as a reference for discussing major theoretical issues, such as the risk that, engaging in this discussion, we reproduce the understanding that the "natural" state of the market is a question of the most efficient liquidity.

Outside academia, Ho's argument has been welcomed not only because it helped to clarify a densely complex issue. The 2007–8 crisis made many members of the public receptive to the idea that financial bankers and their risky strategies—and not abstract, "natural" market forces—has caused many of the hardships they were currently facing. Ho's study offered an insight into the habitus* of risk at the center of a culture where financial bankers are encouraged to take risky decisions for short-term gain, sacrificing any commitment to long-term, stable growth.

Ho's work takes up the baton from previous studies that view financial institutions through an anthropological lens. In her book *The Fools' Gold,* Gillian Tett clarifies that understanding the nature of financial instruments is not sufficient to explain the meltdown of financial institutions. Tett asserts that the financial crisis, rather than being an inevitable result of a financial bubble, has to be explained with reference to the greed of Wall Street bankers. As an academic anthropologist, Ho was able to apply ethnographic methods in her study more comprehensively than Tett, who regards herself "more as an amateur anthropologist than anything else."[7]

The Continuing Debate

As *Liquidated* has generated more consensus than controversy, the book is a continuing source of inspiration, rather than the subject of a continuing debate. An increasing number of authors interested in ethnographic approaches to Wall Street look to *Liquidated* to advance new ideas, identify possible areas of research, and develop new questions.

For example, temporality*—questions involving the organization and the understanding of time—is one aspect of Ho's ethnography currently serving as a reference point for other researchers. The Japanese anthropologist Hirokazu Miyazaki,* for example, "examined a variety of techniques by which [Japanese] derivatives traders sought to reorient themselves in response to temporal incongruities"[8] in their financial activities (different time zones, local working practices and so on). Indeed, the issue of temporality in the financial market is beginning to take shape as a thematic subfield in its own right.

To take another example, the anthropologist Rebecca Cassidy,* referencing a term comparing bankers to gamblers in a casino, argued that "'casino capitalism'* commentators are reinforcing familiar and baseless assumptions about exchange and deflecting serious criticism from the true causes of the problem and how we might respond to them."[9] She is directly inspired by Ho's argument that triumphalist Wall Street discourses*—the discussion of financial matters in terms that emphasize the importance of "victory"—should be critically examined; these discourses grant legitimacy to certain financial strategies, and by examining them, we can shed light on the concrete realities of financial crises, and where the responsibility might lie.

The fact that an increasing number of social scientists are committed to grounding abstract ideas in ethnographic data seems to indicate that anthropology will come to play a role in future debates about the legitimacy of financial capitalism.

NOTES

1   Gillian Tett, "'An Anthropologist on Wall Street,'" Fieldsights—Theorizing
    the Contemporary, *Cultural Anthropology* Online, May 16, 2012, accessed
    October 11, 2015. http://www.culanth.org/fieldsights/362-an-anthropologist-
    on-wall-street.

2   See Hirokazu Miyazaki and Annelise Riles, "Failure as Endpoint," in *Global
    Assemblages: Technology, Politics, and Ethics as Anthropological Problems*,
    ed. Aihwa Ong and Stephen J. Collier (Oxford: Blackwell, 2005), 321.

3   Bill Maurer, "Finance," Fieldsights—Theorizing the Contemporary, *Cultural
    Anthropology* Online, May 01, 2012, accessed October 11, 2015, http://
    www.culanth.org/fieldsights/333-finance.

4   Gillian Tett, "'An Anthropologist on Wall Street.'"

5   Bill Maurer, "The Anthropology of Money," *Annual Review of Anthropology*
    35 (2006):18.

6   "Up w/Chris Hayes," Saturday, June 16, 2012, accessed October 10, 2015,
    http://www.nbcnews.com/id/47864765/ns/msnbc/t/wchris-hayes-saturday-
    june/

7   Tett, "'An Anthropologist on Wall Street.'"

8   Hirokazu Miyazaki, *Arbitraging Japan: Dreams of Capitalism at the End of
    Finance* (Berkeley: University of California Press, 2013), 86.

9   Rebecca Cassidy, "'Casino Capitalism' and the Financial Crisis,"
    Anthropology Today 25, no. 4 (2009): 10.

MODULE 12
WHERE NEXT?

KEY POINTS

- *Liquidated* is already influencing new studies of economic anthropology* and anthropology* of finance.

- Future ethnographers* of finance will be confronted with the same problems that challenged Ho; these problems include the difficult link between the specific methods and subjects used in the discipline of ethnography and the general processes of global finance.

- Ho convincingly pinpoints the main cause of financial crises in the culture of Wall Street,* making an innovative contribution to the anthropology of finance even if she does not necessarily revolutionize it.

Potential

Liquidated: An Ethnography of Wall Street by Karen Z. Ho is already influencing new studies of economic anthropology and the anthropology of finance. The anthropologists Hirokazu Miyazaki* and Rebecca Cassidy* explicitly refer to her work as a major source of inspiration. Ho has contributed to a growing field with a solid, evidence-based book. Her work has strong potential to be of enduring value, and her ideas seem likely to develop in two main directions.

First, *Liquidated* will inspire more academic ethnographies of finance. The book provides an example of how it is possible to use ethnography as an effective method to study financial institutions. Although this is a strategy that has been used in the past, arguably no one before Ho was able to move so expertly from theoretical premises, to methodology, to data collection, to analysis, and draw persuasive conclusions on this basis.

> ❝This close-up portrait of a greedy institution, based on participant observation, is unlikely to be improved upon for a long time. ❞
>
> Mitchel Y. Abolafia, "*Liquidated*"

Second, it can be anticipated that future ethnographers of Wall Street will make an effort to be more accessible to a wider public, while simultaneously trying to base their claims on rigorous methods. Ho made a conscious effort to write accessibly, and succeeded in making an impact beyond academia. However, some critics still judged her language too dense and difficult, making the book tricky for lay readers.

The 2011 *Economist* article, "More Anthropologists on Wall Street, Please,"[1] echoes a growing public sentiment and it seems likely that more anthropologists will answer this call, building on Ho's study with work that considers the cultural and social underpinnings of financial capitalism.*

Future Directions

Ethnographers of finance who use *Liquidated* as a starting point for further research are likely to be confronted with at least some of the problems Ho encountered. The anthropologists Keith Hart* and Horacio Ortiz* point out the limits of "fieldwork-based knowledge," as it is "always haunted by the limits to what one person can observe in a given time and place, [and] this is even more the case with the study of money." They highlight the mysterious and vast nature of financial markets, and express doubts about how deep observation-based methods can go.[2]

Ideally, the future direction of the anthropology of finance would blend the approaches of both ethnographers and grand theorists (those proposing far-reaching theoretical explanations of larger-scale phenomena). Keith Hart and Horacio Ortiz argue that Johns Hopkins University anthropologist Jane Guyer,* in her research on the people of Africa's Atlantic coastal regions, was able to link the local and the global with a combination of long-term participant observation* (observation conducted by people participating in the field of their study), archival research, and historical analysis, thereby moving beyond both "the reductive oversimplifications of economic historians and the parochialism of local ethnographers."[3] Presumably, a future ethnographer of Wall Street could fruitfully apply a similar methodology in order to move beyond *Liquidated* and bring a new contribution to the anthropology of finance.

Summary

In *Liquidated*, Ho illustrates that financial crises are produced by the implementation of financial strategies encouraged by the culture of Wall Street. They do not result from the application of abstract financial models but, rather, are constructed on the basis of social interactions. These social interactions occur in the context of recruitment practices, the workplace, and the relentless pursuit of shareholder value.* It is the culture of liquidity* that predisposes investment bankers* to take risky choices that eventually cause financial collapses. In particular, they are given incentives to bet on the market against all odds because their bonuses rise with the number of transactions they are able to achieve, not their long-term commitment to the stable growth of a company.

Ho's ethnography of Wall Street has been well received both inside and outside academia. She has been praised for her inductive approach* (that is, her logical links between evidence and conclusion), the solidity of her argument, and for the relevance of her analysis for the anthropology of finance and the contemporary debate on financial crises. Minor criticisms targeted her writing style, her arbitrary selection of the historical literature, the confinement of her study to the US case, and her incomplete connection between the culture of Wall Street and the wider processes of global finance.

Despite these gripes, *Liquidated* has already become an influential text in its field. Few anthropologists have been able to establish a compelling connection between culture within sites of financial capital production such as Wall Street and the global processes that make up broader contemporary financial capitalism. Ho's focus on the lived experiences of Wall Streeters and the culture of the finance sector paints a picture of the market as driven by people and their decisions rather than abstract, uncontrollable forces. The ups and downs of the market have a profound impact on society far beyond Wall Street, making anthropology of finance an increasingly relevant field. *Liquidated* seems likely to continue to serve as a springboard for future studies on the cultural foundations of the global financial sector.

NOTES

1   "More Anthropologists on Wall Street Please," *The Economist*, October 24, 2011, accessed October 11, 2015, http://www.economist.com/blogs/democracyinamerica/2011/10/education-policy.

2   Keith Hart and Horacio Ortiz, "The Anthropology of Money and Finance: Between Ethnography and World History," *Annual Review of Anthropology* 43 (2014): 475.

3   Hart and Ortiz, "The Anthropology of Money and Finance," 474.

GLOSSARY

GLOSSARY OF TERMS

Acculturation: the process through which a person acquires the culture of a different group as a consequence of being in contact with its members. It differs from enculturation, which indicates the process of first-culture learning.

American Telephone and Telegraph Incorporated (AT&T): an American multinational corporation in the field of telecommunications. It is the third largest company in Texas.

Anthropology: the systematic study of human beings; while the term commonly refers to the study of beliefs and cultural practices, there are many different branches of anthropological study.

Bankers Trust (BT): a trust company formed by a group of New York national banks. Founded at the beginning of the twentieth century, the company was acquired by Deutsche Bank in 1998 and a number of the staff—including Karen Ho—were downsized.

Black Monday: October 19, 1987, when stock markets around the world experienced a sharp decline in stock prices in a relatively short time.

Capitalism: an economic and social system in which trade, production, and investment are held in private hands and conducted for private profit.

Classical economics: the position, often considered to have been first formulated by the Scottish economist Adam Smith in his book *Wealth of Nations* (1776), that the markets operate best with a minimum of governmental interference.

Corporate America: Karen Z. Ho uses this term "to reference large public corporations throughout the United States and the normative business values and practices that these institutions constructed throughout the twentieth century."

Determinism: the theory that certain inescapable, structural, and pre-existing criteria decide possible given outcomes.

Discourse: the wider "conversation" regarding a specific subject; a system of language and assumptions regarding a specific subject, understood to be interdependent and mutually shaping.

Downsizing: a financial strategy that involves cutting costs by selling off units, laying off employees, and reducing investments in research and development, and infrastructure.

Economic anthropology: a subfield of the discipline of anthropology dealing with economic behavior.

Ethnography: a scientific description of nations, races, or groups of humans, with a particular focus on their customary ideas and practices.

Financial instrument: an asset that can be traded to produce value. Financial instruments include bonds, stocks, derivatives, and many other subcategories.

Formalism: a theoretical approach that tends to represent the economy of any society as made up of individuals who allocate scarce resources to different ends following a standard notion of utility.

Globalization: the process by which people across nations are increasingly interconnected through more rapid and frequent travel communications, and material exchanges.

Habitus: in the work of Pierre Bourdieu, the structure of an individual personality, seen as the composite of dispositions acquired as a result of being immersed in a particular social, cultural context.

Homo economicus: a Latin term that can be translated as "economic man." Economic theorists who consider humans as economically rational, strategic, and self-interested agents often use this term. The "economic man" is not prone to irrational behaviors and is always focused on maximizing his gains.

Inductive reasoning: a series of statements that link evidence and conclusion logically. For example, in *Liquidated* Karen Ho makes a series of statements about Wall Street, which are based on her ethnographic work, and links them to her conclusion that the culture of liquidity produces crises.

Investment bank: a financial institution that provides assistance and consultancy to clients who want to raise their financial capital. Among other services, investment banks assist in mergers and acquisitions, trading of derivatives, and other financial instruments.

Junk bond: a derogatory term to indicate a high-yield bond, which is a financial instrument of indebtedness (of the bond issuer to the holders) with a high risk of not being repaid.

Junk bond crisis: a period of market instability that took place repeatedly between 1980s and 1990s in the US as a consequence of trading high-risk, high-yield financial instruments.

Liquidity: the measure of the speed at which a commodity is bought or sold in the market without affecting the price.

Market temporality: the human perception and organization of time in the particular context of financial markets—its rhythms, working hours, milestones, and so on.

Meritocracy: philosophical position claiming that power, money, and other forms of advantage should only be granted according to individual merit.

Neoclassical economics: an economic approach that supports the rational allocation of resources to alternative ends according to such principles as maximization of utility, use of available knowledge, rational choice, and the independent action of individuals.

Neoliberalism: a body of economic theories in support of privatization, deregulation, free trade, and the enhancement of the private sector at the expense of the public sector. Notable proponents of this view were US president Ronald Reagan and UK prime minister Margaret Thatcher.

Participant observation: a technique used in anthropology in which anthropologists take part in the daily lives of research participants.

Shareholder revolution: a period of time in the 1980s when investment banks started to take over companies with the purpose of breaking them down and selling them on the financial market.

Shareholder value: the wealth earned by the owners of a company's stocks.

Social anthropology: a subfield of anthropology focusing on social behaviors such as economic activity.

Study up: in anthropology, this term refers to a call to apply ethnographic study to dominant or powerful groups, rather than only those on geographical or economic margins, as was historically the case.

Subprime mortgage debacle: the credit emergency in US banks caused by the broad diffusion of subprime loans that, between 2007 and 2008, were not being paid by debtors.

Substantivism: a theoretical idea that sees individual economic actions as influenced by sociocultural factors that vary from context to context.

Temporality: associated with the nature of time; existing inside, or with some specific relationship to, time.

Universalism: a theoretical position that suggests a particular generalization in all possible cases.

Utility: a term used in economics to indicate the measure of satisfaction, advantage, or preference experienced by a subject in return for an economic action. For example, a consumer experiences satisfaction when they perceive the utility of a good or service they have purchased.

Wall Street: Karen Ho conceives of Wall Street as "a cluster of multiply positioned actors who work in the financial services and securities industry" of the US.

PEOPLE MENTIONED IN THE TEXT

Mitchel Abolafia is professor of organizational theory and behavior at the University of Albany. His best-known book *Making Markets* is based on ethnographic research he conducted in Wall Street.

David Akin is professor of anthropology at the University of Michigan. He has conducted research with the Kwaio people of Malaita in the Solomon Islands. One of his most cited publications is a volume he edited with Joel Robbins about the modern uses of local currencies in Melanesia.

Aristotle (384–322 B.C.E.) was a Greek philosopher, scientist, and founder of the Lyceum in Athens. He introduced the idea of "disposition" (*hexis*) in philosophy, which later thinkers developed into the concept of "habitus."

Giovanni Arrighi (1937–2009) was an Italian professor of sociology at Johns Hopkins University. His most famous book, *The Long Twentieth Century*, discusses the origins and transformations of global capitalism.

Maurice Bloch (b. 1939) is a British professor of anthropology at the London School of Economics. He has conducted research in Madagascar and written extensively on political power, cognitive anthropology, and linguistics. With Jonathan Parry, he edited a volume about the difference between "gift" and "commodity."

Pierre Bourdieu (1930–2002) was a French philosopher and sociologist who worked on the concept of symbolic violence and is best known for his work on the reproduction of inequality in French society.

Michel Callon (b. 1945) is professor of sociology at the *École des mines de Paris*. His research focuses on the application of actor-network theory to the study of economic life.

Rebecca Cassidy is professor of anthropology at Goldsmiths College, University of London. She has conducted research on the everyday lives of gamblers in London, and is now working on a project about gambling in Europe.

Thomas Hylland Eriksen (b. 1962) is a Norwegian professor of social anthropology at the University of Oslo and currently president of the European Association of Social Anthropologists. One of his research interests focuses on the popularization of social anthropology.

Chris Gregory (b. 1947) is an Australian anthropologist who conducted research in Papua New Guinea, Fiji, and India. His book *Gifts and Commodities* has become a classic in economic anthropology.

Stephen Gudeman is professor of anthropology at the University of Minnesota. He carried out his research fieldwork in Panama, Colombia, and Guatemala. On the basis of these studies, he has developed his cultural approach to economy, which has comparative aims and cross-disciplinary perspectives.

Jane Guyer (b. 1943) is a Scottish professor of anthropology at Johns Hopkins University. She has conducted research with Atlantic Africans and the relationship between imperialism, development, and global economy.

Keith Hart (b. 1943) is a British anthropologist holding the prestigious position of Centennial Professor of Economic Anthropology at the London School of Economics. He has published widely on economic anthropology, particularly with his research on informal economies in Africa.

Chris Hayes (b. 1979) is an American political commentator hosting a weekday news and opinion television show on American television network MSNBC.

Ellen Hertz is professor of anthropology at the University of Neuchâtel. Her ethnographic research in the Shanghai stock market formed the basis of her best-known book, *The Trading Crowd*.

Bill Maurer is an American anthropologist currently working as dean at the school of social sciences at the University of California, Irvine. His research focuses on money and finance, particularly new and experimental financial instruments.

Marcel Mauss (1872–1950) was a French sociologist, best known for his anthropological book *The Gift*. He wrote an important essay on the concept of "person" (*personne*), which later thinkers used to conceptualize Bourdieu's notion of "habitus."

Philip McMichael is an American sociologist who examines capitalist modernity from the perspective of agrarian studies. He has dealt with the increasing abstraction of the economy as a feature of contemporary global economy.

Daniel Miller (b. 1954) is a professor of material culture at University College London. His research focuses on the relationships between people and things and the consequences of consumption.

Hirokazu Miyazaki is a Japanese anthropologist who holds a position as associate professor of anthropology at Cornell University.

He has conducted ethnographic research among a group of Japanese traders and written about the relationship between finance, culture, and society.

Laura Nader (b. 1930) is an American professor of anthropology at the University of California, Berkeley. In her most quoted publication, "Up the Anthropologist," she encourages anthropologists to "study of the colonizers rather than the colonized, the culture of power rather than the culture of the powerless."

Andrew Orta is professor and head of anthropology at the University of Illinois at Urbana-Champaign. One of his recent projects focuses on the internationalization of business curricula in the United States.

Horacio Ortiz is an anthropologist working at the East China Normal University of Shanghai. He has conducted research with stockbrokers and fund managers in New York and Paris, and is currently working on global financial markets.

Karl Polanyi (1886–1964) was a Hungarian American economist and one of the twentieth century's leading economic historians. He is the author of *The Great Transformation: The Political and Economic Origins of our Time* and is considered to be the originator of substantivism.

Joel Robbins is Sigrid Rausing Professor of Social Anthropology at the University of Cambridge. His research interests span from religion to economy, with a focus on Papua New Guinea. He edited a volume with David Akin about the local meaning of currencies in Melanesia.

Stuart Alexander Rockefeller is a visiting scholar at the Center for the Study of Ethnicity and Race at Columbia University. He has conducted ethnography in a rural community in the Bolivian Andes.

Marshall Sahlins (b. 1930) is an American emeritus professor of anthropology at the University of Chicago and a central reference in the field of economic anthropology. His best-known book, *Stone Age Economics*, is a collection of essays on human economies studied with a substantivist perspective.

Don Slater is associate professor of sociology at the London School of Economics. His research focuses on material consumption, new media, and development.

Gillian Tett (b. 1967) is a British writer and journalist at the *Financial Times* who specializes in markets and finance. Her best-known book, *The Fool's Gold*, deals with the 2007–8 financial crisis and won the Spear's Book Award for the financial book of 2009.

Fran Tonkiss is professor of sociology at the London School of Economics. She has conducted research in economic sociology, with a focus on global markets and social capital.

WORKS CITED

WORKS CITED

Abolafia, Mitchel Y. "*Liquidated: An Ethnography of Wall Street* by Karen Ho." *American Journal of Sociology* 116, no. 1 (2010): 272–3.

— — —. *Making Markets: Opportunism and Restraint on Wall Street.* Cambridge, Mass.: Harvard University Press, 2001.

Appadurai, Arjun, ed. *The Social Life of Things: Commodities in Cultural Perspective.* Cambridge: Cambridge University Press, 1988.

Arrighi, Giovanni. *The Long Twentieth Century: Money, Power, and the Origins of Our Times.* London: Verso, 1994.

Blackford, Mansel G. "*Liquidated: An Ethnography of Wall Street.*" *The Business History Review* 85, no. 3 (2011): 627–9.

Braithwaite, John, and Peter Drahos. "Globalization of Corporate Regulation and Corporate Citizenship." In *International Corporate Law*, vol. 2, edited by Fiona MacMillan, 3–44. Portland, OR: Hart Publishing, 2003.

Callon, Michel. "Introduction: The Embeddedness of Economic Markets in Economics." In *The Laws of the Markets*, edited by Michael Callon, 1–57. Oxford: Blackwell Publishers, 1998.

Carrier, James G., ed. *Meanings of the Market: The Free Market in Western Culture.* Oxford: Berg, 1997.

Caruso, Giuseppe. "*Liquidated. An Ethnography of Wall Street* by Karen Ho." *The Experience of Collective Action.* May 17, 2011. Accessed October 11, 2015. https://giuseppecaruso.wordpress.com/2011/05/17/liquidated-an-ethnography-of-wall-street-by-karen-ho/.

Cassidy, Rebecca. "'Casino Capitalism' and the Financial Crisis." *Anthropology Today* 25, no. 4 (2009): 10–13.

Cox, Alexandra B. "Making Markets and Constructing Crises: A Review of Ho's *Liquidated.*" *The Qualitative Report* 17 (2012): 1–4.

Dalton, George. "Economic Theory and Primitive Society." *American Anthropologist* 63, no. 1 (1961): 1–25.

Eriksen, Thomas Hylland. *Engaging Anthropology: The Case for a Public Presence.* Oxford: Berg, 2006.

Graeber, David. *Debt: The First 5,000 Years.* Brooklyn, NY: Melville House, 2012.

Gudeman, Stephen. *Economics as Culture: Models and Metaphors of Livelihood.* Boston: Routledge and Kegan Paul, 1986.

Hart, Keith. "Contemporary Research on the Anthropology of Money and Finance." *The Memory Bank.* September 4, 2013. Accessed October 9, 2015. http://thememorybank.co.uk/2013/09/04/contemporary-research-on-the-anthropology-of-money-and-finance/.

— — —. "Review of *Liquidated: An Ethnography of Wall Street* by Karen Ho." *American Ethnologist* 38, no. 2 (May 1, 2011): 378–9.

Hart, Keith, and Horacio Ortiz. "The Anthropology of Money and Finance: Between Ethnography and World History." *Annual Review of Anthropology* 43 (2014): 465–82.

Ho, Karen Z. "Commentary on Andrew Orta's 'Managing the Margins': The Anthropology of Transnational Capitalism, Neoliberalism, and Risk." *American Ethnologist* 41, no. 1 (2014): 31–7.

— — —. "Disciplining Investment Bankers, Disciplining the Economy: Wall Street's Institutional Culture of Crisis and the Downsizing of 'Corporate America.'" *American Anthropologist* 111, no. 2 (2009): 177–89.

— — —. "Finance." In *Encyclopedia of Social and Cultural Anthropology, 2nd Ed.,* edited by Alan Barnard and Jonathan Spencer, 295–8. London and New York: Routledge, 2010.

— — —. *Liquidated: An Ethnography of Wall Street.* Durham: Duke University Press, 2009.

— — —. "Situating Global Capitalisms: A View from Wall Street Investment Banks." *Cultural Anthropology* 20, no. 1 (2005): 68–96.

Maurer, Bill. "The Anthropology of Money." *Annual Review of Anthropology* 35 (2006): 15–36.

— — —. "Finance." Fieldsights—Theorizing the Contemporary. *Cultural Anthropology* Online. May 01, 2012. Accessed October 11, 2015. http://www.culanth.org/fieldsights/333-finance.

— — —. *Mutual Life, Limited: Islamic Banking, Alternative Currencies, Lateral Reason.* Princeton, N.J.: Princeton University Press, 2005.

McMichael, Philip. "Development and Structural Adjustment." In *Virtualism: A New Political Economy*, edited by James G. Carrier and Daniel Miller, 95–116. Oxford: Berg, 1998.

Miller, Daniel. "Turning Callon the Right Way Up." *Economy and Society* 31, no. 2 (2002): 218–33.

Miyazaki, Hirokazu. "The Temporalities of the Market." *American Anthropologist* 105, no. 2 (2003): 255–65.

—— —. *Arbitraging Japan: Dreams of Capitalism at the End of Finance.* Berkeley: University of California Press, 2013.

Miyazaki, Hirokazu, and Annelise Riles. "Failure as Endpoint." In *Global Assemblages: Technology, Politics, and Ethics as Anthropological Problems,* edited by Aihwa Ong and Stephen J. Collier, 320–31. Oxford: Blackwell, 2005.

"More Anthropologists on Wall Street Please." *The Economist,* October 24, 2011. Accessed October 11, 2015. http://www.economist.com/blogs/democracyinamerica/2011/10/education-policy.

Nader, Laura. "Up the Anthropologist—Perspectives Gained from Studying Up." In *Reinventing Anthropology*, edited by Dell Hymes, 284–311. New York: Pantheon Books, 1972.

"Nonfiction Book Review: *Liquidated: An Ethnography of Wall Street* by Karen Zouwen Ho." PublishersWeekly.com. Accessed October 10, 2015. http://www.publishersweekly.com/978-0-8223-4599-2.

Orta, Andrew. "Cultures of Capitalism, Contexts of Capitalism (Reply to Karen Ho)." *American Ethnologist* 41, no. 1 (2014), 39.

Polanyi, Karl. *The Great Transformation: The Political and Economic Origins of Our Time.* Boston: Beacon Press, 1944.

Rockefeller, Stuart Alexander. "Flow." *Current Anthropology* 52, no. 4 (2011): 557–78.

Sahlins, Marshall. *Stone Age Economics.* New York: Aldine, 1972.

Slater, Don, and Fran Tonkiss. *Market Society: Markets and Modern Social Theory.* Oxford: Polity Press, 2001.

Tett, Gillian. "'An Anthropologist on Wall Street.'" Fieldsights—Theorizing the Contemporary. *Cultural Anthropology* Online. May 16, 2012. Accessed October 11, 2015. http://www.culanth.org/fieldsights/362-an-anthropologist-on-wall-street.

—— —. "Books of the Year: Gems among a string of credit-crunch tomes." *Management Today.* December 1, 2009. Accessed October 9, 2015. http://www.managementtoday.co.uk/news/969289/Books-Year-Gems-among-string-credit-crunch-tomes/?DCMP=ILC-SEARCH.

"'Up w/Chris Hayes' for Saturday, June 16, 2012." Accessed October 10, 2015. http://www.nbcnews.com/id/47864765/ns/msnbc/t/wchris-hayes-saturday-june/.

THE MACAT LIBRARY
BY DISCIPLINE

AFRICANA STUDIES

Chinua Achebe's *An Image of Africa: Racism in Conrad's Heart of Darkness*
W. E. B. Du Bois's *The Souls of Black Folk*
Zora Neale Huston's *Characteristics of Negro Expression*
Martin Luther King Jr's *Why We Can't Wait*
Toni Morrison's *Playing in the Dark: Whiteness in the American Literary Imagination*

ANTHROPOLOGY

Arjun Appadurai's *Modernity at Large: Cultural Dimensions of Globalisation*
Philippe Ariès's *Centuries of Childhood*
Franz Boas's *Race, Language and Culture*
Kim Chan & Renée Mauborgne's *Blue Ocean Strategy*
Jared Diamond's *Guns, Germs & Steel: the Fate of Human Societies*
Jared Diamond's *Collapse: How Societies Choose to Fail or Survive*
E. E. Evans-Pritchard's *Witchcraft, Oracles and Magic Among the Azande*
James Ferguson's *The Anti-Politics Machine*
Clifford Geertz's *The Interpretation of Cultures*
David Graeber's *Debt: the First 5000 Years*
Karen Ho's *Liquidated: An Ethnography of Wall Street*
Geert Hofstede's *Culture's Consequences: Comparing Values, Behaviors, Institutes and Organizations across Nations*
Claude Lévi-Strauss's *Structural Anthropology*
Jay Macleod's *Ain't No Makin' It: Aspirations and Attainment in a Low-Income Neighborhood*
Saba Mahmood's *The Politics of Piety: The Islamic Revival and the Feminist Subject*
Marcel Mauss's *The Gift*

BUSINESS

Jean Lave & Etienne Wenger's *Situated Learning*
Theodore Levitt's *Marketing Myopia*
Burton G. Malkiel's *A Random Walk Down Wall Street*
Douglas McGregor's *The Human Side of Enterprise*
Michael Porter's *Competitive Strategy: Creating and Sustaining Superior Performance*
John Kotter's *Leading Change*
C. K. Prahalad & Gary Hamel's *The Core Competence of the Corporation*

CRIMINOLOGY

Michelle Alexander's *The New Jim Crow: Mass Incarceration in the Age of Colorblindness*
Michael R. Gottfredson & Travis Hirschi's *A General Theory of Crime*
Richard Herrnstein & Charles A. Murray's *The Bell Curve: Intelligence and Class Structure in American Life*
Elizabeth Loftus's *Eyewitness Testimony*
Jay Macleod's *Ain't No Makin' It: Aspirations and Attainment in a Low-Income Neighborhood*
Philip Zimbardo's *The Lucifer Effect*

ECONOMICS

Janet Abu-Lughod's *Before European Hegemony*
Ha-Joon Chang's *Kicking Away the Ladder*
David Brion Davis's *The Problem of Slavery in the Age of Revolution*
Milton Friedman's *The Role of Monetary Policy*
Milton Friedman's *Capitalism and Freedom*
David Graeber's *Debt: the First 5000 Years*
Friedrich Hayek's *The Road to Serfdom*
Karen Ho's *Liquidated: An Ethnography of Wall Street*

John Maynard Keynes's *The General Theory of Employment, Interest and Money*
Charles P. Kindleberger's *Manias, Panics and Crashes*
Robert Lucas's *Why Doesn't Capital Flow from Rich to Poor Countries?*
Burton G. Malkiel's *A Random Walk Down Wall Street*
Thomas Robert Malthus's *An Essay on the Principle of Population*
Karl Marx's *Capital*
Thomas Piketty's *Capital in the Twenty-First Century*
Amartya Sen's *Development as Freedom*
Adam Smith's *The Wealth of Nations*
Nassim Nicholas Taleb's *The Black Swan: The Impact of the Highly Improbable*
Amos Tversky's & Daniel Kahneman's *Judgment under Uncertainty: Heuristics and Biases*
Mahbub Ul Haq's *Reflections on Human Development*
Max Weber's *The Protestant Ethic and the Spirit of Capitalism*

FEMINISM AND GENDER STUDIES

Judith Butler's *Gender Trouble*
Simone De Beauvoir's *The Second Sex*
Michel Foucault's *History of Sexuality*
Betty Friedan's *The Feminine Mystique*
Saba Mahmood's *The Politics of Piety: The Islamic Revival and the Feminist Subject*
Joan Wallach Scott's *Gender and the Politics of History*
Mary Wollstonecraft's *A Vindication of the Rights of Woman*
Virginia Woolf's *A Room of One's Own*

GEOGRAPHY

The Brundtland Report's *Our Common Future*
Rachel Carson's *Silent Spring*
Charles Darwin's *On the Origin of Species*
James Ferguson's *The Anti-Politics Machine*
Jane Jacobs's *The Death and Life of Great American Cities*
James Lovelock's *Gaia: A New Look at Life on Earth*
Amartya Sen's *Development as Freedom*
Mathis Wackernagel & William Rees's *Our Ecological Footprint*

HISTORY

Janet Abu-Lughod's *Before European Hegemony*
Benedict Anderson's *Imagined Communities*
Bernard Bailyn's *The Ideological Origins of the American Revolution*
Hanna Batatu's *The Old Social Classes And The Revolutionary Movements Of Iraq*
Christopher Browning's *Ordinary Men: Reserve Police Batallion 101 and the Final Solution in Poland*
Edmund Burke's *Reflections on the Revolution in France*
William Cronon's *Nature's Metropolis: Chicago And The Great West*
Alfred W. Crosby's *The Columbian Exchange*
Hamid Dabashi's *Iran: A People Interrupted*
David Brion Davis's *The Problem of Slavery in the Age of Revolution*
Nathalie Zemon Davis's *The Return of Martin Guerre*
Jared Diamond's *Guns, Germs & Steel: the Fate of Human Societies*
Frank Dikotter's *Mao's Great Famine*
John W Dower's *War Without Mercy: Race And Power In The Pacific War*
W. E. B. Du Bois's *The Souls of Black Folk*
Richard J. Evans's *In Defence of History*
Lucien Febvre's *The Problem of Unbelief in the 16th Century*
Sheila Fitzpatrick's *Everyday Stalinism*

Eric Foner's *Reconstruction: America's Unfinished Revolution, 1863-1877*
Michel Foucault's *Discipline and Punish*
Michel Foucault's *History of Sexuality*
Francis Fukuyama's *The End of History and the Last Man*
John Lewis Gaddis's *We Now Know: Rethinking Cold War History*
Ernest Gellner's *Nations and Nationalism*
Eugene Genovese's *Roll, Jordan, Roll: The World the Slaves Made*
Carlo Ginzburg's *The Night Battles*
Daniel Goldhagen's *Hitler's Willing Executioners*
Jack Goldstone's *Revolution and Rebellion in the Early Modern World*
Antonio Gramsci's *The Prison Notebooks*
Alexander Hamilton, John Jay & James Madison's *The Federalist Papers*
Christopher Hill's *The World Turned Upside Down*
Carole Hillenbrand's *The Crusades: Islamic Perspectives*
Thomas Hobbes's *Leviathan*
Eric Hobsbawm's *The Age Of Revolution*
John A. Hobson's *Imperialism: A Study*
Albert Hourani's *History of the Arab Peoples*
Samuel P. Huntington's *The Clash of Civilizations and the Remaking of World Order*
C. L. R. James's *The Black Jacobins*
Tony Judt's *Postwar: A History of Europe Since 1945*
Ernst Kantorowicz's *The King's Two Bodies: A Study in Medieval Political Theology*
Paul Kennedy's *The Rise and Fall of the Great Powers*
Ian Kershaw's *The "Hitler Myth": Image and Reality in the Third Reich*
John Maynard Keynes's *The General Theory of Employment, Interest and Money*
Charles P. Kindleberger's *Manias, Panics and Crashes*
Martin Luther King Jr's *Why We Can't Wait*
Henry Kissinger's *World Order: Reflections on the Character of Nations and the Course of History*
Thomas Kuhn's *The Structure of Scientific Revolutions*
Georges Lefebvre's *The Coming of the French Revolution*
John Locke's *Two Treatises of Government*
Niccolò Machiavelli's *The Prince*
Thomas Robert Malthus's *An Essay on the Principle of Population*
Mahmood Mamdani's *Citizen and Subject: Contemporary Africa And The Legacy Of Late Colonlulism*
Karl Marx's *Capital*
Stanley Milgram's *Obedience to Authority*
John Stuart Mill's *On Liberty*
Thomas Paine's *Common Sense*
Thomas Paine's *Rights of Man*
Geoffrey Parker's *Global Crisis: War, Climate Change and Catastrophe in the Seventeenth Century*
Jonathan Riley-Smith's *The First Crusade and the Idea of Crusading*
Jean-Jacques Rousseau's *The Social Contract*
Joan Wallach Scott's *Gender and the Politics of History*
Theda Skocpol's *States and Social Revolutions*
Adam Smith's *The Wealth of Nations*
Timothy Snyder's *Bloodlands: Europe Between Hitler and Stalin*
Sun Tzu's *The Art of War*
Keith Thomas's *Religion and the Decline of Magic*
Thucydides's *The History of the Peloponnesian War*
Frederick Jackson Turner's *The Significance of the Frontier in American History*
Odd Arne Westad's *The Global Cold War: Third World Interventions And The Making Of Our Times*

LITERATURE

Chinua Achebe's *An Image of Africa: Racism in Conrad's Heart of Darkness*
Roland Barthes's *Mythologies*
Homi K. Bhabha's *The Location of Culture*
Judith Butler's *Gender Trouble*
Simone De Beauvoir's *The Second Sex*
Ferdinand De Saussure's *Course in General Linguistics*
T. S. Eliot's *The Sacred Wood: Essays on Poetry and Criticism*
Zora Neale Huston's *Characteristics of Negro Expression*
Toni Morrison's *Playing in the Dark: Whiteness in the American Literary Imagination*
Edward Said's *Orientalism*
Gayatri Chakravorty Spivak's *Can the Subaltern Speak?*
Mary Wollstonecraft's *A Vindication of the Rights of Women*
Virginia Woolf's *A Room of One's Own*

PHILOSOPHY

Elizabeth Anscombe's *Modern Moral Philosophy*
Hannah Arendt's *The Human Condition*
Aristotle's *Metaphysics*
Aristotle's *Nicomachean Ethics*
Edmund Gettier's *Is Justified True Belief Knowledge?*
Georg Wilhelm Friedrich Hegel's *Phenomenology of Spirit*
David Hume's *Dialogues Concerning Natural Religion*
David Hume's *The Enquiry for Human Understanding*
Immanuel Kant's *Religion within the Boundaries of Mere Reason*
Immanuel Kant's *Critique of Pure Reason*
Søren Kierkegaard's *The Sickness Unto Death*
Søren Kierkegaard's *Fear and Trembling*
C. S. Lewis's *The Abolition of Man*
Alasdair MacIntyre's *After Virtue*
Marcus Aurelius's *Meditations*
Friedrich Nietzsche's *On the Genealogy of Morality*
Friedrich Nietzsche's *Beyond Good and Evil*
Plato's *Republic*
Plato's *Symposium*
Jean-Jacques Rousseau's *The Social Contract*
Gilbert Ryle's *The Concept of Mind*
Baruch Spinoza's *Ethics*
Sun Tzu's *The Art of War*
Ludwig Wittgenstein's *Philosophical Investigations*

POLITICS

Benedict Anderson's *Imagined Communities*
Aristotle's *Politics*
Bernard Bailyn's *The Ideological Origins of the American Revolution*
Edmund Burke's *Reflections on the Revolution in France*
John C. Calhoun's *A Disquisition on Government*
Ha-Joon Chang's *Kicking Away the Ladder*
Hamid Dabashi's *Iran: A People Interrupted*
Hamid Dabashi's *Theology of Discontent: The Ideological Foundation of the Islamic Revolution in Iran*
Robert Dahl's *Democracy and its Critics*
Robert Dahl's *Who Governs?*
David Brion Davis's *The Problem of Slavery in the Age of Revolution*

Alexis De Tocqueville's *Democracy in America*
James Ferguson's *The Anti-Politics Machine*
Frank Dikotter's *Mao's Great Famine*
Sheila Fitzpatrick's *Everyday Stalinism*
Eric Foner's *Reconstruction: America's Unfinished Revolution, 1863-1877*
Milton Friedman's *Capitalism and Freedom*
Francis Fukuyama's *The End of History and the Last Man*
John Lewis Gaddis's *We Now Know: Rethinking Cold War History*
Ernest Gellner's *Nations and Nationalism*
David Graeber's *Debt: the First 5000 Years*
Antonio Gramsci's *The Prison Notebooks*
Alexander Hamilton, John Jay & James Madison's *The Federalist Papers*
Friedrich Hayek's *The Road to Serfdom*
Christopher Hill's *The World Turned Upside Down*
Thomas Hobbes's *Leviathan*
John A. Hobson's *Imperialism: A Study*
Samuel P. Huntington's *The Clash of Civilizations and the Remaking of World Order*
Tony Judt's *Postwar: A History of Europe Since 1945*
David C. Kang's *China Rising: Peace, Power and Order in East Asia*
Paul Kennedy's *The Rise and Fall of Great Powers*
Robert Keohane's *After Hegemony*
Martin Luther King Jr.'s *Why We Can't Wait*
Henry Kissinger's *World Order: Reflections on the Character of Nations and the Course of History*
John Locke's *Two Treatises of Government*
Niccolò Machiavelli's *The Prince*
Thomas Robert Malthus's *An Essay on the Principle of Population*
Mahmood Mamdani's *Citizen and Subject: Contemporary Africa And The Legacy Of Late Colonialism*
Karl Marx's *Capital*
John Stuart Mill's *On Liberty*
John Stuart Mill's *Utilitarianism*
Hans Morgenthau's *Politics Among Nations*
Thomas Paine's *Common Sense*
Thomas Paine's *Rights of Man*
Thomas Piketty's *Capital in the Twenty-First Century*
Robert D. Putman's *Bowling Alone*
John Rawls's *Theory of Justice*
Jean-Jacques Rousseau's *The Social Contract*
Theda Skocpol's *States and Social Revolutions*
Adam Smith's *The Wealth of Nations*
Sun Tzu's *The Art of War*
Henry David Thoreau's *Civil Disobedience*
Thucydides's *The History of the Peloponnesian War*
Kenneth Waltz's *Theory of International Politics*
Max Weber's *Politics as a Vocation*
Odd Arne Westad's *The Global Cold War: Third World Interventions And The Making Of Our Times*

POSTCOLONIAL STUDIES

Roland Barthes's *Mythologies*
Frantz Fanon's *Black Skin, White Masks*
Homi K. Bhabha's *The Location of Culture*
Gustavo Gutiérrez's *A Theology of Liberation*
Edward Said's *Orientalism*
Gayatri Chakravorty Spivak's *Can the Subaltern Speak?*

PSYCHOLOGY

Gordon Allport's *The Nature of Prejudice*
Alan Baddeley & Graham Hitch's *Aggression: A Social Learning Analysis*
Albert Bandura's *Aggression: A Social Learning Analysis*
Leon Festinger's *A Theory of Cognitive Dissonance*
Sigmund Freud's *The Interpretation of Dreams*
Betty Friedan's *The Feminine Mystique*
Michael R. Gottfredson & Travis Hirschi's *A General Theory of Crime*
Eric Hoffer's *The True Believer: Thoughts on the Nature of Mass Movements*
William James's *Principles of Psychology*
Elizabeth Loftus's *Eyewitness Testimony*
A. H. Maslow's *A Theory of Human Motivation*
Stanley Milgram's *Obedience to Authority*
Steven Pinker's *The Better Angels of Our Nature*
Oliver Sacks's *The Man Who Mistook His Wife For a Hat*
Richard Thaler & Cass Sunstein's *Nudge: Improving Decisions About Health, Wealth and Happiness*
Amos Tversky's *Judgment under Uncertainty: Heuristics and Biases*
Philip Zimbardo's *The Lucifer Effect*

SCIENCE

Rachel Carson's *Silent Spring*
William Cronon's *Nature's Metropolis: Chicago And The Great West*
Alfred W. Crosby's *The Columbian Exchange*
Charles Darwin's *On the Origin of Species*
Richard Dawkin's *The Selfish Gene*
Thomas Kuhn's *The Structure of Scientific Revolutions*
Geoffrey Parker's *Global Crisis: War, Climate Change and Catastrophe in the Seventeenth Century*
Mathis Wackernagel & William Rees's *Our Ecological Footprint*

SOCIOLOGY

Michelle Alexander's *The New Jim Crow: Mass Incarceration in the Age of Colorblindness*
Gordon Allport's *The Nature of Prejudice*
Albert Bandura's *Aggression: A Social Learning Analysis*
Hanna Batatu's *The Old Social Classes And The Revolutionary Movements Of Iraq*
Ha-Joon Chang's *Kicking Away the Ladder*
W. E. B. Du Bois's *The Souls of Black Folk*
Émile Durkheim's *On Suicide*
Frantz Fanon's *Black Skin, White Masks*
Frantz Fanon's *The Wretched of the Earth*
Eric Foner's *Reconstruction: America's Unfinished Revolution, 1863-1877*
Eugene Genovese's *Roll, Jordan, Roll: The World the Slaves Made*
Jack Goldstone's *Revolution and Rebellion in the Early Modern World*
Antonio Gramsci's *The Prison Notebooks*
Richard Herrnstein & Charles A Murray's *The Bell Curve: Intelligence and Class Structure in American Life*
Eric Hoffer's *The True Believer: Thoughts on the Nature of Mass Movements*
Jane Jacobs's *The Death and Life of Great American Cities*
Robert Lucas's *Why Doesn't Capital Flow from Rich to Poor Countries?*
Jay Macleod's *Ain't No Makin' It: Aspirations and Attainment in a Low Income Neighborhood*
Elaine May's *Homeward Bound: American Families in the Cold War Era*
Douglas McGregor's *The Human Side of Enterprise*
C. Wright Mills's *The Sociological Imagination*

Thomas Piketty's *Capital in the Twenty-First Century*
Robert D. Putman's *Bowling Alone*
David Riesman's *The Lonely Crowd: A Study of the Changing American Character*
Edward Said's *Orientalism*
Joan Wallach Scott's *Gender and the Politics of History*
Theda Skocpol's *States and Social Revolutions*
Max Weber's *The Protestant Ethic and the Spirit of Capitalism*

THEOLOGY

Augustine's *Confessions*
Benedict's *Rule of St Benedict*
Gustavo Gutiérrez's *A Theology of Liberation*
Carole Hillenbrand's *The Crusades: Islamic Perspectives*
David Hume's *Dialogues Concerning Natural Religion*
Immanuel Kant's *Religion within the Boundaries of Mere Reason*
Ernst Kantorowicz's *The King's Two Bodies: A Study in Medieval Political Theology*
Søren Kierkegaard's *The Sickness Unto Death*
C. S. Lewis's *The Abolition of Man*
Saba Mahmood's *The Politics of Piety: The Islamic Revival and the Feminist Subject*
Baruch Spinoza's *Ethics*
Keith Thomas's *Religion and the Decline of Magic*

COMING SOON

Chris Argyris's *The Individual and the Organisation*
Seyla Benhabib's *The Rights of Others*
Walter Benjamin's *The Work Of Art in the Age of Mechanical Reproduction*
John Berger's *Ways of Seeing*
Pierre Bourdieu's *Outline of a Theory of Practice*
Mary Douglas's *Purity and Danger*
Roland Dworkin's *Taking Rights Seriously*
James G. March's *Exploration and Exploitation in Organisational Learning*
Ikujiro Nonaka's *A Dynamic Theory of Organizational Knowledge Creation*
Griselda Pollock's *Vision and Difference*
Amartya Sen's *Inequality Re-Examined*
Susan Sontag's *On Photography*
Yasser Tabbaa's *The Transformation of Islamic Art*
Ludwig von Mises's *Theory of Money and Credit*

Macat Disciplines

Access the greatest ideas and thinkers across entire disciplines, including

FEMINISM, GENDER AND QUEER STUDIES

Simone De Beauvoir's
The Second Sex

Michel Foucault's
History of Sexuality

Betty Friedan's
The Feminine Mystique

Saba Mahmood's
*The Politics of Piety:
The Islamic Revival and
the Feminist Subject*

Joan Wallach Scott's
*Gender and the
Politics of History*

Mary Wollstonecraft's
*A Vindication of the
Rights of Woman*

Virginia Woolf's
A Room of One's Own

Judith Butler's
Gender Trouble

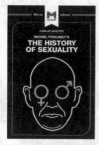

Macat analyses are available from all good bookshops and libraries.

Access hundreds of analyses through one, multimedia tool.
Join free for one month **library.macat.com**

Macat Disciplines

Access the greatest ideas and thinkers across entire disciplines, including

INEQUALITY

Ha-Joon Chang's, *Kicking Away the Ladder*

David Graeber's, *Debt: The First 5000 Years*

Robert E. Lucas's, *Why Doesn't Capital Flow from Rich To Poor Countries?*

Thomas Piketty's, *Capital in the Twenty-First Century*

Amartya Sen's, *Inequality Re-Examined*

Mahbub Ul Haq's, *Reflections on Human Development*

Macat analyses are available from all good bookshops and libraries.

Access hundreds of analyses through one, multimedia tool.
Join free for one month **library.macat.com**

Macat Disciplines

Access the greatest ideas and thinkers across entire disciplines, including

GLOBALIZATION

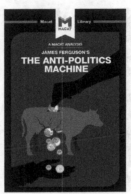

Arjun Appadurai's, *Modernity at Large: Cultural Dimensions of Globalisation*

James Ferguson's, *The Anti-Politics Machine*

Geert Hofstede's, *Culture's Consequences*

Amartya Sen's, *Development as Freedom*

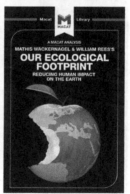

Macat Pairs

Analyse historical and modern issues from opposite sides of an argument. Pairs include:

RACE AND IDENTITY

Zora Neale Hurston's
Characteristics of Negro Expression

Using material collected on anthropological expeditions to the South, Zora Neale Hurston explains how expression in African American culture in the early twentieth century departs from the art of white America. At the time, African American art was often criticized for copying white culture. For Hurston, this criticism misunderstood how art works. European tradition views art as something fixed. But Hurston describes a creative process that is alive, ever-changing, and largely improvisational. She maintains that African American art works through a process called 'mimicry'—where an imitated object or verbal pattern, for example, is reshaped and altered until it becomes something new, novel—and worthy of attention.

Frantz Fanon's
Black Skin, White Masks

Black Skin, White Masks offers a radical analysis of the psychological effects of colonization on the colonized.

Fanon witnessed the effects of colonization first hand both in his birthplace, Martinique, and again later in life when he worked as a psychiatrist in another French colony, Algeria. His text is uncompromising in form and argument. He dissects the dehumanizing effects of colonialism, arguing that it destroys the native sense of identity, forcing people to adapt to an alien set of values—including a core belief that they are inferior. This results in deep psychological trauma.

Fanon's work played a pivotal role in the civil rights movements of the 1960s.

Macat Pairs

Analyse historical and modern issues from opposite sides of an argument. Pairs include:

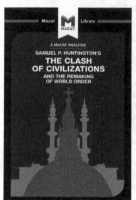

Macat Pairs

*Analyse historical and modern issues
from opposite sides of an argument.
Pairs include:*

ARE WE FUNDAMENTALLY GOOD - OR BAD?

Steven Pinker's
The Better Angels of Our Nature

Stephen Pinker's gloriously optimistic 2011 book argues that, despite humanity's biological tendency toward violence, we are, in fact, less violent today than ever before. To prove his case, Pinker lays out pages of detailed statistical evidence. For him, much of the credit for the decline goes to the eighteenth-century Enlightenment movement, whose ideas of liberty, tolerance, and respect for the value of human life filtered down through society and affected how people thought. That psychological change led to behavioral change—and overall we became more peaceful. Critics countered that humanity could never overcome the biological urge toward violence; others argued that Pinker's statistics were flawed.

Philip Zimbardo's
The Lucifer Effect

Some psychologists believe those who commit cruelty are innately evil. Zimbardo disagrees. In *The Lucifer Effect*, he argues that sometimes good people do evil things simply because of the situations they find themselves in, citing many historical examples to illustrate his point. Zimbardo details his 1971 Stanford prison experiment, where ordinary volunteers playing guards in a mock prison rapidly became abusive. But he also describes the tortures committed by US army personnel in Iraq's Abu Ghraib prison in 2003—and how he himself testified in defence of one of those guards. committed by US army personnel in Iraq's Abu Ghraib prison in 2003—and how he himself testified in defence of one of those guards.

Macat analyses are available from all good bookshops and libraries.

Access hundreds of analyses through one, multimedia tool.
Join free for one month **library.macat.com**

Macat Pairs

Analyse historical and modern issues from opposite sides of an argument. Pairs include:

HOW WE RELATE TO EACH OTHER AND SOCIETY

Jean-Jacques Rousseau's
The Social Contract

Rousseau's famous work sets out the radical concept of the 'social contract': a give-and-take relationship between individual freedom and social order.

If people are free to do as they like, governed only by their own sense of justice, they are also vulnerable to chaos and violence. To avoid this, Rousseau proposes, they should agree to give up some freedom to benefit from the protection of social and political organization. But this deal is only just if societies are led by the collective needs and desires of the people, and able to control the private interests of individuals. For Rousseau, the only legitimate form of government is rule by the people.

Robert D. Putnam's
Bowling Alone

In *Bowling Alone*, Robert Putnam argues that Americans have become disconnected from one another and from the institutions of their common life, and investigates the consequences of this change.

Looking at a range of indicators, from membership in formal organizations to the number of invitations being extended to informal dinner parties, Putnam demonstrates that Americans are interacting less and creating less "social capital" – with potentially disastrous implications for their society.

It would be difficult to overstate the impact of *Bowling Alone*, one of the most frequently cited social science publications of the last half-century.

Printed in the United States
by Baker & Taylor Publisher Services